W9-CFB-465

Edited by Catherine Marjoribanks
Copyedited by Tanya Trafford
Proofread by Judy Phillips
Designed by Belle Wuthrich
First edition edited by Pam Robertson

Annick Press Ltd.

We acknowledge the support of the Canada Council for the Arts, the Ontario Arts
Council, and the participation of the Government of Canada/la participation du
gouvernement du Canada for our publishing activities.

ONTARIO ARTS COUNCIL
CONSEIL DES ARTS DE L'ONTARIO
an Ontario government agency
un organisme du gouvernement de l'Ontario

Funded by the
Government
of Canada

Financé par le
gouvernement
du Canada

Canadä

Cataloging in Publication
Lee, Cora, author   The great number rumble : a story of math in
surprising places / Cora Lee & Gillian O'Reilly. — Revised edition.

Includes bibliographical references and index.
Issued in print and electronic formats.
ISBN 978-1-55451-849-4 (paperback).—ISBN 978-1-55451-850-0 (hardcover)

1. Mathematics—Juvenile literature. I. O'Reilly, Gillian, author II. Title.
QA40.5.L47 2016   j510   C2016-900559-3

Distributed in Canada by University of Toronto Press.
Published in the U.S.A. by Annick Press (U.S.) Ltd.
Distributed in the U.S.A. by Publishers Group West.

Printed in China

Visit us at: www.annickpress.com
Visit Lil Crump at: ideahousedesign.com

Also available in e-book format.
Please visit www.annickpress.com/ebooks.html for more details. Or scan

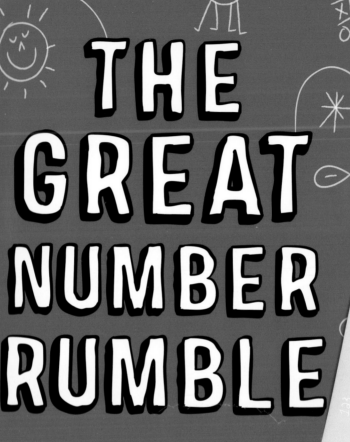

THE GREAT NUMBER RUMBLE

A STORY OF MATH IN SURPRISING PLA

Cora Lee & Gillian O'Reilly

annick press
toronto + berkeley + vancouver

TABLE OF CONTENTS

For Jaime and Peter, of course—and Hayley, Alyssa, Anna, Ben, Chloe, and Justin, new mathematicians in the making.

—CL

For my father, who appreciates both numbers and words and who made Möbius strips for all our birthday parties.

—GO'R

—CL and GO'R

Thanks to Nancy Rawlinson, Jim O'Reilly, Dora Lee, Evan Lee, Stan Jang, Loris Lesynski, and Alan and Ian Usher for their help at various points along the way.

For Rachael C., my favorite always. Thanks to B.C. and to my ever-supportive family. And thanks, Ceilidh, for incessantly forcing me to take micro-breaks.

—LC

NO MORE MATH!

MY FRIEND SAM, he's crazy about math. Me (the name's Jeremy), I can do without it. Math has nothing to do with me, and I have nothing to do with it—except when it comes to homework, and then I'm the kind of guy who desperately needs a calculator. At least, that's what I thought until we had our big math debate or, as I like to call it, "The Great Number Rumble." That was the day when…but wait, first some introductions.

Sam was still new to the neighborhood when The Number Rumble happened. At first, I thought he was just like me: tall, dark, and good-looking. Well, except that I've got red hair and freckles. And, okay, "good-looking" might be wishful thinking. But we liked to do a lot of the same things—ride bikes, listen to music, watch movies.

There was one major, *major* difference, though—he was nuts about numbers and anything else to do with math.

SAM   JEREMY

SAM		JEREMY
→ dark-haired	→ messy	→ red-haired
→ number-nutty	→ likes bikes,	→ freckled
→ algebra-crazy	sports,	→ skateboarder
→ fractal-fixated	video games,	→ rollerblader
→ geometry-loving	movies,	→ comic & thriller
→ fantasy & mystery	music	reader
reader		→ plays guitar
→ plays keyboard		→ joker

NEITHER: GOOD-LOOKING

VENN? VHAT? VHERE? A Venn diagram is a way of showing how sets (or groups) of things called elements are related. Every element in the first circle, Set Sam, is what makes Sam, Sam. Set Jeremy in the other circle is all about...wait for it...Jeremy! How are they even friends? That's what the intersection of the sets, where the circles overlap, shows: they do have some things in common! And what does the space outside both circles tell you? Only the truth...what they're not.

     Not that he spent all summer studying or anything. From the day we met, we goofed around a lot—swimming, biking, playing video games. Or Sam looked up skateboard trivia while I practiced my jumps. Sometimes we just flopped out on the couch and read—mystery novels for Sam, comics for me. Pretty soon, he was just Sam to me. A regular guy who saw the world differently—as numbers, shapes, and patterns.

When we started school, everyone thought Sam was either a genius or a geek, and didn't really know what to make of him. But the kids (knowing what a great judge of character I am) soon accepted him, even if they didn't always understand him. Sam prefers the word "mathnik"—he thinks it describes all of us, in fact, not just him. No way, I said, not me. But Sam says we were all born that way, no matter how far some of us (*cough!*) have strayed. I wasn't so sure about that, but there's no arguing with the guy.

JEREMY WRESTLES WITH THE WEIRD STUFF

SAM SAYS THAT SCIENTISTS have proven that babies recognize differences in the numbers of things—only two days after they're born! According to these scientists, then, when I was a baby I'd get bored seeing picture after picture showing two dots, no matter how the dots were arranged, but I'd get excited as soon as you switched to a picture of three dots. When I was a few months older I could tell the difference between bigger numbers like 8 and 16. At five months I'd get upset if you tried to show me that 1 toy plus 1 toy equaled 3, and at nine months, I knew that 5 + 5 = 10!

Pretty smart back then, wasn't I? So... what happened?

Anyway, Sam's low-key about his talent—doesn't make a big deal about it. "Math is nothing special," he's always saying. "It's everywhere and in everything, and we all use it all the time, not just me."

Well, one day, he had to prove it. Because the last thing we ever expected to happen… happened. It all started with one tweet from a reporter that went viral.

Apparently, the director of education, Lawrence Lake, was removing mathematics from the school curriculum, effective immediately.

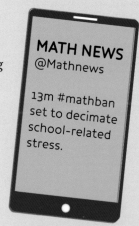

MATH NEWS
@Mathnews

13m #mathban set to decimate school-related stress.

YOU HEARD ME, VIRAL. And no, you didn't sleep through Math and wake up in Biology. When a tweet goes viral, it spreads the way the flu does, but faster (what's quicker, a retweet or a sneeze?). It's called exponential growth: 1 tweet gets, say, 20 retweets, and each of those gets 20 more, and so on, and so on. Tweets rarely run wild enough to reach epidemic status, though. So while going viral is a medical nightmare, it's only a twitterer's daydream.

When he heard the news, Sam lost it. He was so mad, he threw on yesterday's clothes that were lying around the room (hey, mathniks dump their clothes on the floor just like the rest of us) and ran right over to my place. That tells you how upset he was. Normally, when it comes to his wardrobe he's the mix 'n' match master—he consults this big chart on his computer for different mathematical combinations, and he can go almost a whole year without wearing the same thing twice.

WHAT DO YOU MEAN, nothing to wear? Even with just 2 T-shirts, 4 pairs of jeans, and 2 pairs of shoes, you've got 16 outfit options!

Sam just about exploded through the door at my house. "Jeremy! Did you hear? No more math!"

"I won't lie—sounds good to me," I responded. Of course, that only made him madder.

"Are you kidding? Geometry and graphs, gone. In all probability, no probability! How could they do this?"

He ranted all the way to school. I didn't understand half of what he was talking about—algorithms, logarithms, iterations, tessellations— but whatever, I just let him get it out of his system.

When we got there, it was a circus. Talk about chaos! Recycling bins full of math texts and notebooks, kids everywhere tossing out their rulers, even their calculators! Teachers too. You should have seen the grin on Ms. Norton's face. I always knew she hated teaching math.

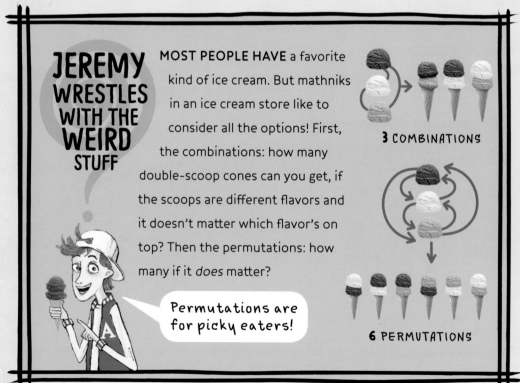

JEREMY WRESTLES WITH THE WEIRD STUFF

MOST PEOPLE HAVE a favorite kind of ice cream. But mathniks in an ice cream store like to consider all the options! First, the combinations: how many double-scoop cones can you get, if the scoops are different flavors and it doesn't matter which flavor's on top? Then the permutations: how many if it *does* matter?

Permutations are for picky eaters!

3 COMBINATIONS

6 PERMUTATIONS

The news cameras were there too.

Someone thrust a microphone in my face. "What do you think of the ban, kid? I guess you're pleased, eh?"

"I've got no problem with it," I said.

"Are you kidding?" Sam shoved me aside. "The idea is crazy! Does the director have any idea how much we would all lose if he goes through with the ban? Math is worth learning about for so many reasons! If I had just one afternoon with Mr. Lake, I'd show him just how much he needs it!"

"Great idea," cut in Ms. Kay, the school librarian. "Why don't we organize a little debate right here at our school? It would be an excellent learning opportunity…for young Samuel and Jeremy, and the other kids, of course."

JEREMY WRESTLES WITH THE WEIRD STUFF

SAM'S ALWAYS GETTING ON MY CASE about the word "chaos." When I use it, I mean a huge, confused mess! But Sam says that in mathematics, chaos is something that's perfectly logical underneath, even though the situation is always changing and impossible to predict. That's because tiny changes at the start make a huge difference in the end. It's called the "butterfly effect." In weather systems, for example, the air stirred by a butterfly's wing can trigger changes that lead, months down the road, to a hurricane halfway around the world! The same thing happens with a pinball machine—the tiniest difference in how you launch the ball changes its route in a major way.

PYTHAGORAS

(c. 560–480 BCE)

ALL IS NUMBER. The Greek philosopher and mathematician couldn't have picked a more perfect motto for his semi-scientific secret society. Its rules were strict—take a sacred oath of secrecy, own nothing, live as a group, and eat no meat, for starters. But the goal was simple: find proof that the universe is based on whole numbers.

The Pythagoreans wore the five-pointed star, and reached some pretty bizarre conclusions—that numbers had personalities and genders, for example. But other discoveries were brilliant: harmonious ratios, triangle numbers, square numbers, and the famous Pythagorean theorem ($a^2 + b^2 = c^2$), which describes the relationship between the sides of *any* right triangle. Not bad for a guy who had to bribe his first student to listen to him!

Evidence for a mathematical universe was growing (or so the members of the Order believed). But then, disaster struck. A Pythagorean named Hippasus discovered the square root of two, which was impossible to write as a ratio of whole numbers. A cover-up ensued, then murder, as Hippasus betrayed his oath of secrecy and was drowned by fanatic Pythagoreans. After Pythagoras himself died, the Order weakened and eventually self-destructed.

Ha! I guess it really does pay to stay in school!

WHAT IS MATH? Mathematics is making sense of amounts, shapes, and space. It's exploring how these kinds of things link up and fit together in patterns. It's way more than just numbers. So, what is math? The real question is: what isn't?

The reporter agreed, and whipped out her phone to call the director of education to ask if he would come to the school to meet with a concerned student. The reporter hung up and nodded at us. "He laughed, but he said he'd be happy to come by during lunch. Guess I'll see you back here at noon, then."

I glanced at Ms. Kay as we left. Why did she look so pleased?

GAME ON, MATH-LETES!

WORD GOT OUT FAST. When Sam and I walked into the gym at noon, it was almost full: besides the reporters, a TV crew, our teachers, the principal and vice principal, and the director of education, there were tons of kids.

"Hey, Sam, you know how *you* like math, but me, not so much?" I began. "Well, I think way more people are like me than like you. And the director hates math for sure. So, how are you going to convince him?"

"No worries," he answered, "I've got a plan. *And* a backup plan."

I wasn't sure I wanted his plan to work, whatever it was. Still, Sam's my friend; I didn't want him to look stupid either. Shrugging, I followed him through the crowd and grabbed a seat up front to catch all the action.

Ms. Kay introduced Sam and Mr. Lake to the crowd and asked the director to speak first. He stepped up to the mike, smiling to the audience.

"Well, well," he said to Sam. "I hear you have some concerns about my decision to remove math from the curriculum. So, what is it—you're going to miss irrational and imaginary numbers? Who needs them when we have enough trouble with real ones, right?" He looked around to see how we liked his little joke. "All you kids need is basic arithmetic, anyway: adding, subtracting, multiplication, and division. Maybe not even those. After all, isn't that what calculators are for? Or is it word problems you think you'll miss? I promise you, you won't need those. When was the last time anyone told you he was eight years younger than four times the square root of your sister's age?"

JEREMY WRESTLES WITH THE WEIRD STUFF

A NUMBER'S A NUMBER, RIGHT? *Wrong*, says Sam.

Natural numbers: Numbers you can count on! 1, 2, 3...

Whole numbers: 0, 1, 2, 3... Early Europeans thought the Indian idea of zero was evil: after all, how could you write nothing?

Integers: Whole numbers with negative numbers (...-3, -2, -1, 0, 1, 2, 3...)

Rational numbers: Numbers you can write as decimals (0.25) or fractions, which are ratios of two whole numbers (1/2). Rational, ratios...get it?

Irrational numbers: Numbers you can't write as a fraction or as a decimal, because they never end and show no logical repeating pattern—like pi (π, or 3.141592653...) or the square root of 2 (written as $\sqrt{2}$ or 1.41421356...), which was so...well, irrational, it got Hippasus killed!

Imaginary numbers: The real deal! Real numbers times the imaginary "i," invented to find the square roots of negative numbers, which is logically impossible with real numbers.

Whoa! Stop right there! Why can't we be like the Pirahã tribe in Brazil, and just use one, two and many?

12

You could tell the director thought he was being clever. He went on: "Don't be afraid to speak up, son. I'm sure I can help you appreciate the correct point of view."

"I doubt it," said Sam, not smiling. "In fact, I'm so sure that you've made the wrong decision that I propose a little bet."

"A bet?" chuckled the director.

"Yes," said Sam. "I'm going to convince you and everyone here that math is not only important but exciting too, and part of everything we do. And if I can't change your mind, I promise to work for you every day after school for the whole year."

WILL SAM WIN HIS BET? What are the chances? Probability is like good guessing: it's the math that measures how likely something is to happen. A sure thing has a probability of one, but if there's no way it's happening, the probability is zero. A number in between means some degree of "maybe." If it's so iffy that it could go either way, the probability is 0.5 or, as they say, 50-50. Stay tuned...

"For free? Don't get too confident now," said the director.

I let out a whistle...this was a high-stakes bet for Sam!

"Well, no. I was going to suggest that you pay me one cent a day for the first day, then double it to two cents the second, four cents the third, eight cents the fourth, and so on."

"You certainly won't get rich that way," laughed the director. "But sure, it's a deal."

The director shook Sam's hand and returned to his chair with a smug smile. I saw the vice principal open his mouth to say something, but then he closed it when he caught Ms. Kay's eye. She winked at him and he winked back. Something was definitely going on. I just couldn't figure out what it was.

JEREMY WRESTLES WITH THE WEIRD STUFF

Oh great. More kinds of numbers?

→ **Palindrome number:** a number that reads the same backwards and forwards, like 626 or 147,741.

→ **Perfect number:** a number that equals the sum of its factors, not including itself. Six is a perfect number: 1 + 2 + 3 = 6.

→ **Square number:** the product of a number multiplied by itself, like 4 = 2 x 2, aka 2 squared—it even looks like a square!

0	1	4	9	16

→ **Triangle number:** a number calculated by totaling whole numbers in order. Examples: 0 + 1 = 1, 1 + 2 = 3, 1 + 2 + 3 = 6, 1 + 2 + 3 + 4 = 10—stack them to make triangles, or add next-door triangle numbers to get square numbers!

0	1	3	6	10

"All right, let's start right here in the gym," said Sam, getting comfortable in front of the mike.

"Are you sure, son? Not much math here!"

Sam just looked at him calmly. "There's math right in front of you." Sam waved over our friend Emily. She had just returned to the school after a training ride for her next bike race.

"Hey, Sam. Hello, Mr. Lake," she said, leaning her bike against the wall. "How am I supposed to help? I mean, math's okay, but it's got nothing to do with me."

"Sure it does," Sam said. "Biking is math—it's geometry in motion."

And with that, the great debate was on.

"Almost all bike frames have triangles in them—because that's the strongest shape there is," continued Sam. "The triangles won't collapse under the rider's weight, even with all the bumps, braking, and hard pedaling. It's the same reason you see triangles in bridges, skyscrapers, and geodesic domes."

MOUNTAIN BIKES are made for off-road riding—barreling through streams and jolting over rocks. The short, wide triangle means you ride low, and are more stable and less likely to tip.

A BMX is built to fly! A super-skinny back triangle means you're really close to the ground and super stable. That means better control over tilting when you're jumping, spinning, and flying around a track full of bumps, jumps, and berms.

ROAD BIKES are built with tall, thin triangles for long, smooth rides or races. They don't have to be low because there's no need to twist, turn, or jump. Tipping isn't much of an issue, and you have lots of leg room for comfortable pedaling.

"Too bad that doesn't help me get up the hills any easier," I said, thinking about my trip home after school. "I never make it to the top without stopping."

"Actually, some geometry can help you there, too—circles this time, and their ratios," replied Sam.

"Okay...the wheels are circles," I said. "And, duh, circles roll. But up a hill, they want to roll backwards!"

"I don't mean the wheels," said Sam. "I mean the whole pedal-gear-chain setup—it's inspired! The gear ratio compares the sizes of the front and back gears, which control how many times your wheel goes around with each turn of the pedals. A high gear ratio (big front gear, small back one) gets you more turns of the wheel each time you turn the pedal."

"High gears are perfect for riding on flat roads, when pushing hard to cover more ground is okay," added Emily.

"Right," said Sam. "Not like up a hill. Then, who cares about distance? Gear down quick, for a low gear ratio (small front gear, big back gear) and sacrifice ground covered for easier riding."

What did I tell you? Everything is a shape or a pattern to Sam. For him, a bike was all triangles and circles.

BACK GEAR

CHAIN

FRONT GEAR

JEREMY WRESTLES WITH THE WEIRD STUFF

WHAT DO YOU CALL A BIKE with square wheels? Useless—ha ha! But seriously, Sam told me about a mathematics professor named Stan Wagon who actually built a bike with square wheels! Of course, he had to build his own road, too. It had evenly spaced bumps of just the right size and shape, what he called "inverted catenaries." A catenary is the curve you get when, for example, you let a skipping rope or a chain hang with an end in each of your hands. Imagine a row of these upside down, and Professor Wagon's weird wheels rolling over it.

Pentagonal (five-sided) wheels roll on inverted-catenary roads too, but the bumps have to be flatter and shorter in length. Hexagonal (six-sided) wheels need even smaller bumps. In fact, the more sides a wheel has, the flatter and shorter the bumps have to be. So what do you get if you keep on adding sides? You guessed it—a round wheel on a flat road!

Emily was fascinated—she loves knowing the science behind what she does. But Mr. Lake wasn't too impressed. "A bike is a bike," he said. "And getting up a hill takes simple, hard work—not thinking about a lot of numbers and shapes."

Sam was ready with another example. "There's math in basketball, too," he said, grabbing a ball from a bin nearby. "You can make more baskets by simply adjusting the angle of your launch. And if angles aren't math, I don't know what is.

"Angles are useful when you're punting a football; throwing a ball, javelin, or discus; or even winging a water balloon! And, from where I'm standing," Sam continued, lobbing the ball into the basket with a swoosh, "this angle is perfect."

"That's all cool," said Emily. Some of the other kids jumped up and started trying to perfect their free throws by shooting basketballs at low, medium, and high angles. The gym was pretty noisy for a minute, but the vice principal, who always carries a very loud whistle, brought us back to order quickly.

"Sorry," said Mr. Lake, shaking his head. "You'll have to do better than that if you're going to convince me that math is part of *everything* we do. How many kids are serious enough about sports to actually use math?"

"You know something?" said Sam with a grin, "you're right. The serious athletes are a small percentage of the whole, and a wider survey might better reflect the majority. You just used statistics to support your argument!"

Several kids giggled. It *was* funny. According to Sam, the director was using math, without even knowing it, to tell us we shouldn't let a small group like the sports nuts speak for the rest of us.

WHAT GOES UP, MUST COME DOWN... Sir Isaac Newton said it first. But there's more: the rise and fall of a basketball follows a parabola shape. At first it travels both up and away, but then gravity wins out and the ball starts falling. How far it gets depends a lot on the angle you launch the ball at.

If you shoot at an angle that's too low—and nothing else about your shot changes—then gravity will drag the ball down before it gets very far.

If you launch high, it goes a long way up, but only a short way forward.

Turns out that a medium angle—45 degrees—gets you the best distance, if that's what you're after.

ARCHIMEDES

(c. 287–212 BCE)

THE GREEK MATHEMATICIAN ARCHIMEDES made discoveries about pi and the volumes and surface areas of spheres and cylinders, invented valuable weapons of war, and even gave us a catchy phrase for whenever a brilliant idea hits. The sight of water overflowing from the tub as he got into his bath one day sparked the solution to a tricky problem. The king of Syracuse wanted to know if his new gold crown was real, or just a gold-plated rip-off. Archimedes realized that a silver-and-gold fake would displace, or spill out, more water than a pure gold crown. He was so excited he jumped out of the tub and raced naked through the streets shouting "Eureka!" (I've found it!)

Could he be any smarter? An old manuscript says yes! When scientists used modern methods to recover the words hidden under an old prayer book, they discovered more of Archimedes's ideas. Clearly, he had understood infinity and even calculus—a math supposedly invented almost 2,000 years after his death. Sadly, it was his love of math that got Archimedes killed. When Syracuse was captured by the Romans, an impatient soldier ran a sword through the old man when he insisted on solving his geometry problem before following him.

Those close to Archimedes always hoped that his next great discovery would be the bath mat.

Mr. Lake frowned, then looked suspiciously at Sam. "Statistics? I'm sure I meant no such thing. All I'm saying is that we must keep things in perspective, look at the big picture."

"Did you say picture?"

It was Oscar. Uh-oh. This wasn't going to be good for Sam. Where Sam was all about numbers and logic, Oscar was all creativity and emotion. He was great at art, bad at math—and didn't care who knew it.

"Better step away if you want your math back, Sammy," Oscar said. "Art and math, they don't mix. Math is just numbers—it's got nothing to do with art."

"You'd be surprised," replied Sam.

Wait, where was he going with this now? I figured I was about to find out, because Sam was leading us out of the gym!

A MATH-STERPIECE

SAM LED US INTO THE ART ROOM—well, as many of us as could crowd in. I was confused—it sure looked like a math-free zone to me.

"What are we doing in here?" asked Oscar, sneering. "Maybe you're thinking preschool—that's where you just make pretty patterns. Real artists don't work like that."

"M. C. Escher's a real artist, isn't he?" asked Sam, pointing to a poster on the wall.

"Maurits Cornelis Escher?" said Oscar. "Of course he's a real artist—a great 20th-century graphic artist—that's *artist,* not mathematician," he emphasized.

"True," said Sam. "Escher wasn't a mathematician. But check out his art: it's loaded with math. A lot of his mind-bending illusions use tessellations, like this one with intertwined green, red, and white fish." At my puzzled look, he added, "Shapes that *tessellate* fit together perfectly with no gaps or overlaps. You want to lock them together so there aren't any gaps, like my sneaker tread, or the pattern on a soccer ball."

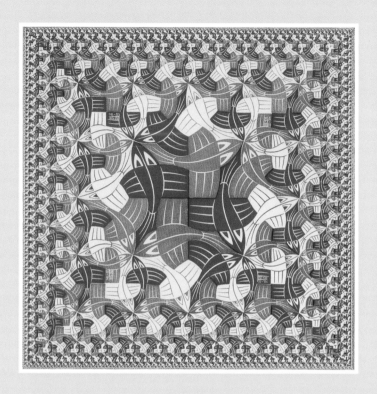

"You're comparing Escher's art to your sneaker tread?" Oscar asked in disbelief.

"Not exactly. The simplest tessellations are—" began Sam. "Wait...I'll show you." He walked over to an art table loaded with supplies and started cutting out a shape from a big piece of foam. "Jeremy, grab that paint—let's make some art."

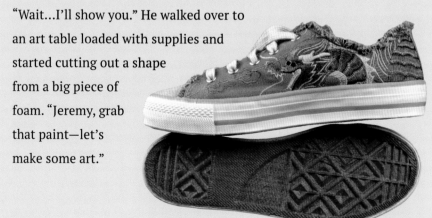

DIY: EASY ESCHER!

Supplies: scissors, tape, two jars of paint (different colors), poster paper, and a bag of craft foam

1. Cut a squiggly shape from one side of a foam square and tape it to the opposite side. (Anything you cut from one side has to go back on the other.)

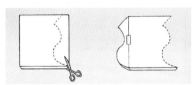

2. Cut another shape from the bottom and tape it to the top.

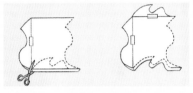

3. Trace the finished shape onto another foam piece, and cut out a copy (the two pieces should fit together on all sides).

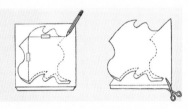

4. Dip one foam shape into a jar of paint and stamp the shape at the top left corner of the poster paper.

5. Dip the other copy into the other jar of paint and stamp it next to the first imprint.

6. Repeat, switching colors each time, stamping side by side and down the page.

There! Six steps to your own math-sterpiece!

Sam kept talking while we cut and dipped and stamped.

"Like I was saying, the simplest tessellations are made from just one shape with the same size angles and sides all around, like a triangle, square, or hexagon. The ones made from two or more shapes are a bit more complicated. And then there's Escher—but even his most complex illusions started with simple shapes."

"That's no Escher," said Oscar, barely looking at our masterpiece.

JEREMY WRESTLES WITH THE WEIRD STUFF

ALGORITHMS RULE. They don't just give computers step-by-step instructions, they tell me what to do! When I look up something using Google, the search engine gives me the best websites first, ranking them by calculating how often other web pages, especially "important" or highly ranked ones, link to them.

Amazon uses algorithms to calculate the similarity between pairs of items bought or rated by a customer, and groups them together. Then, when I buy one thing, Amazon politely recommends more of the same.

Facebook's algorithm is pretty bossy. It doesn't even ask what I want; it just finds stuff posted by my better buds—especially videos, photos, and trendy topics—and puts them higher in my newsfeed.

Everything I get online now is mathematically tailored to me... "like" it or not!

ACCORDING TO UNIVERSITY OF TORONTO mathematician Donald Coxeter, Escher drew all the crisscrossing arcs in his *Circle Limit III* perfectly, with no knowledge of the trigonometric calculations that others might need to construct them!

"But, yeah, okay, I'll give you that—it's math. Whatever. That's graphic art. I'm more into art that looks real, where math doesn't matter at all."

"Are you kidding? What about CGI? Some of the most realistic stuff in animated or live action movies is made using computer-generated images," said Sam. "Have you seen *Big Hero 6?* San Fransokyo could totally be a real city. There's no limit to what an animator and an algorithm can do!"

"No limit? Uh, I hope not," I said. "I mean, there isn't a movie monster alive (so to speak) that can spook me—but show me a life-like, computer-generated human being, and I totally freak."

Sam laughed. "That's the 'Uncanny Valley' effect, what some roboticists and animators use to describe the idea of how we like artificial humans, but only to a point. I guess when they become both too human, and not quite human enough, our puny brains can't take it! So we banish them to the Uncanny Valley."

"Where they live on, if only in our nightmares," I added. "Glad it's not just me."

"Yeah, CGI is pretty cool...but you're right, there *is* a lot of math behind it," said Oscar. "Good thing I can always count on this!" He held up his sketchpad and a pencil. "This is all I need to draw portraits, landscapes, comics. In fact, I kind of like manga right now. And there's a bonus: no math required."

STUDIOS SUCH AS PIXAR and DreamWorks use animation algorithms to build pixel-perfect worlds so real, it's unreal. Here's how:

1. **Create a digital scene:** use equations to connect millions of geometric shapes into skeletons for each character and object.

2. **Make them move**—animators have three main methods to mimic movement, which requires 24 to 60 images, or frames, per second:
   → keyframing lets the animator fix an object's shape and position at key points—then the computer figures out what goes in between
   → procedural animation uses algorithms to force everything—from computer-generated fire and smoke to water, clothes, hair, and rocks—to follow the laws of physics, and to make artificial life-forms act real
   → motion capture uses computers to record real actors moving, and fit this data to digital characters (see below)

3. **Lighten up:** computers have to calculate every bounce and bump each time light contacts a surface that's a different color or texture.

4. **Finally, piece millions of digital art parts** into the final product.

One computer working pixel by pixel is too slow, so many powerful computers do the work together, in groups called "render farms."

HYPATIA OF ALEXANDRIA

(c. 370–415 CE)

THE DAUGHTER of the mathematician Theon, Hypatia grew up to become not only an important public speaker and philosopher but the greatest mathematician and astronomer of her time! She was a popular teacher at the university in Alexandria, in Egypt, famous for its huge libraries. And legend says she was so beautiful that she taught from behind a screen so she wouldn't distract her students.

It was the wrong time and place to be so outstanding, though. A growing number of Christians in Alexandria were suspicious of any religious ideas or philosophies that did not support their own beliefs. One night, a mob of fanatical monks attacked Hypatia on her way home. They dragged her to a church, hacked her to pieces, and burned her remains. Some historians call this event the start of the Dark Ages for Europe, when institutions such as the library at Alexandria were destroyed and Greek and Roman knowledge disappeared for some 1,000 years.

TIME FOR A REALITY CHECK. Look at the numbers it took to get this movie done!

How to Train Your Dragon 2 (2014, DreamWorks)

1,409 frames per minute. For this 92-minute movie, that's 129,600 frames!

495 artists

90 million **render hours** (that would take one computer 10,273 years!)

700 million **digital files totaling 398 terabytes of memory**

"Any kind of drawing, even comics, uses math," said Sam. He stepped up to the flip chart next to the art teacher's desk. "Think about it. It's a 3-D world, but the paper you draw on is only 2-D. So how do you get from this," Sam said, drawing a square on the chart, "to that?" He pointed to an illustration of a cube tacked to the wall near the Escher prints.

"That's perspective," said Oscar. "Not math."

"Back in the 15th century," explained Sam, "the Renaissance artists—who were also mathematicians, scientists, and musicians, by

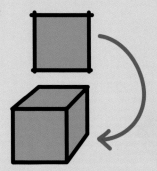

MATHEMATICAL RULES can lead to some pretty fancy folding. Physicist-engineer-origami artist Robert Lang invented a computer program for folding amazing paper people, moose, even scorpions and insects. Engineers use origami algorithms to make leak-proof paper pots, stuff airbags into cars, and tightly pack 100-meter (328-foot) telescope lenses to send into space. And Transformers aren't just toys anymore: using origami folding patterns and materials that fold on contact with, say, heat or water, researchers have invented four-legged robots that can transform from a single, flat wafer in minutes, and minibots the size of a sugar cube that can walk, swim, and climb. One day we might have medical minibots small enough to enter the human body, unfold, and make repairs before dissolving away.

the way—started noticing that things appeared to change in size and shape depending on where you stood. So they did all the math—"

"You're not listening," Oscar interrupted. "All you need to know is perspective!"

"—and then they translated their results into a system of clues called *perspective*, which is what you use to do all your comics and other drawings. A new math called projective geometry grew out of this method," finished Sam.

Oscar turned bright red. *Ha!* Now Sam handed him the marker. "Draw us a scene from one of your comics," he said. "Manga, super-heroes, whatever. We can look for vanishing points and see if your geometry checks out."

"There—not bad!" said Sam. "Looks like you're a mathematician after all."

RHYTHM OR ALGORITHM?

NOW, SAM'S A SMART GUY. But sometimes, he just doesn't get it, especially where people are concerned. And telling Oscar he was a mathematician...well, that was definitely a mistake.

"An artist's genius and a mathematician's brain!" Oscar was admiring his own work—you could say he was giving us his own *perspective* on his perspective. "No wonder I'm so good!"

See what I mean? Luckily, Oscar's show-off session was cut short by Jen.

"Don't think you're the only artist-mathematician here," she said, rolling her eyes. "There's plenty of math in music, too."

"Huh?" said Oscar.

Jen's crazy about music—she and her friends have their own band, and sometimes they let me jam with them, until I go overboard on the guitar riffs. She likes math, too. And Sam can play a mean keyboard when he puts his mind to it, so when Jen and Sam get going, watch out! It's like math and music rule the universe.

"Music and math *belong* together!" she said. "Your Renaissance artists knew it. Even people back in the Middle Ages knew it! I can't believe you don't see the connection." Jen was getting so intense that Oscar started backing away. "The four classes you absolutely had to take in medieval universities were arithmetic, geometry, astronomy, and *music*." She turned to confront Mr. Lake. "That's what *we* should do. Instead of taking away math, you should be adding more music!"

Mr. Lake looked around helplessly.

"A lot of early mathematicians were trained musicians, too," added Sam. "It's easy to see why."

"It is?" Mr. Lake squeaked out the question.

"Of course it is," said an exasperated Jen. "Tempo, motifs, time signatures...even harmony is based in math. I'll show you."

Jen led everyone across the hall to the music room. She grabbed from a stand the first sheet of music she saw, pulled another from her own bag, and thrust both into Mr. Lake's hands.

"Jeremy? Are we boring you?" Jen asked in a polite but dangerous voice.

Busted! I had been making my way quietly to the back of the room to check out the new guitars. "Sorry!" (Hey, in my defense, I never stick to the script, musical or otherwise! I like to improvise—ask my teachers.)

"Never mind," she sighed. "You're going to use that guitar to make some math. Remember Pythagoras? He used math and a monochord— kind of a prehistoric guitar—to figure out what notes sounded good together. Pluck any string on that guitar and you get one note, right?

ROCKING IT, PYTHAGORAS STYLE! Good vibrations don't happen by chance. There's a pattern to what notes are "consonant," or sound good together. On a guitar, pressing different frets shortens a string into different lengths, producing different sounds. If you pluck the same string on two different guitars together, you get consonance (harmony) when the string lengths are ratios of small whole numbers.

Jeremy plucks the top string of the guitar—this is called an open string.

Jen presses on different frets on the guitar.

1

1

Open string + open string (1:1 string-length ratio) = unison

1

1/2

Open string + half a string (2:1 string-length ratio) = octave

1

2/3

Open string + two thirds string (3:2 string-length ratio) = fifth

1

63/81

Open string + 63/81 string = OUCH!

CONSONANCE!

But you get dissonance (clashing sounds) when the string lengths are not ratios of small whole numbers.

Now hold down that same string exactly halfway down the neck and pluck it again. It vibrates twice as fast and you hear it an octave higher."

"Okay," I said. "This first string is E." I plucked it a few times. "Now, if I count *exactly* halfway down the frets...see, that sounds like E too, but an octave higher! What do you think of this?"

I gave my best imitation of Pythagoras as a rock musician playing with just those two notes.

"Go back to the first E and keep plucking," Jen said, picking up a second guitar and trying a few different notes. "See how these sound good together? You get the best sounds when my string is a whole-number ratio of yours—that's when you get octaves (2:1), fifths (3:2), and fourths (4:3)."

Then I tried some random fancy fingering, which got me some weird clashing chords! "Nope, I don't think there's a future for a band called Pythagoras and the Rockin' Ratios."

"Right," said Jen dryly, taking the guitar away from me. "That noise you're making is the result of some wildly non-whole-number ratios.

YOUR MP3 PLAYER SQUEEZES a hefty 32-megabyte song down to a mere 3 megabytes by mathematically stripping out parts of the sound signal that you don't need, replacing extra-long or duplicate bits with shorter code. (Newer MP4 technology does the same with video, text, and pictures.)

You might not be impressed, but to Pythagoras, the results from these string experiments were proof that ratios of small whole numbers ruled the world."

"That's all well and good for those of you taking music lessons," interrupted Mr. Lake, "but I'm not convinced that it makes math necessary. I myself never had music lessons, and I don't think very many of us are destined to become composers!"

JEREMY WRESTLES WITH THE WEIRD STUFF

HOW CAN MUSICAL RATIOS rule the world? Well, those ratios included the same small whole numbers—1, 2, 3, and 4—that the Pythagoreans were so nuts about! It was like evidence for their version of the universe, with a perfectly spherical Sun, Earth, and other planets circling precisely around each other, separated by harmonic ratios of distances, and singing in perfect harmony! Were they psychic or what? Space probes have brought back evidence that the energy surrounding stars causes measurable sound vibration near their surfaces. Three of Earth's nearby celestial bodies are apparently sounding out some eerie tunes, and a super-massive black hole in the Perseus Cluster is belting out a B-flat, 57 octaves below middle C. And what about that modern physics idea, superstring theory, which says tiny vibrating strings make up our world?

How did Pythagoras know?

> **Using math to make music is nothing new.**

LONG BEFORE MIDI TECHNOLOGY existed, people were using probability theory to chop up other composers' work and remake it as their own. And the guys doing it 300 years ago didn't need computers, just a pair of dice, some scissors, and a manual titled *A Tabular System Whereby the Art of Composing Minuets Is Made So Easy That Any Person, without the Least Knowledge of Musick, May Compose Ten Thousand, All Different, and in the Most Pleasing and Correct Manner*—a *Composing for Dummies* of sorts, for those wannabes in 1775. All the "composer" had to do was number the bars on a sheet of music written by someone else, cut them out, and rearrange them randomly. It was like hip-hop sampling, except that hip-hop artists choose what they want to use, while in the 1700s they used dice or other random-number generators to arrange the bits. Sneaky move! Probability theory was still pretty new, but these guys knew the chances of getting the exact same pattern of pieces were really, really low—so they could always count on rolling out an "original"!

> **I love it! The slice-and-dice method of composing!**

> **5-minute music masterpieces #♥Pinterest**

If Beethoven were alive today!

The man had a point. Only musical geniuses could compose their own music, right? I was thinking Sam was stuck this time—

"Not true," said Sam. "MIDI keyboards make it simple enough for anyone to compose."

But of course I was wrong. Leave it to the math master!

"With a MIDI keyboard, you can write music for a ton of different instruments, program a backup band, and experiment with different tempos and effects. It records and prints out music for you, too," continued Sam.

"And the math?" asked Mr. Lake, frowning.

"I was getting to that," replied Sam. "The keyboard understands only MIDI numbers—"

"Musical Instrument Digital Interface numbers," offered Jen, seeing the puzzled look on Mr. Lake's face.

"Thanks," said Sam. "So each time you press a key, you're putting musical instructions into code. One number is the note you're playing, another says how loud or how long, and another indicates the instrument you've chosen. When you play it back, the numbers are decoded and turned back into sounds, which are already built into the keyboard. So it's really not music being recorded, it's math."

MUHAMMAD IBN MUSA AL-KHWARIZMI

(c. 780–850 CE)

SOLVE FOR A: $3 + a = 5$. What about $a^2 + 1 = 26$? Or $2a^2 + 2a = 24$? If you can solve these questions, thank Muhammad ibn Musa al-Khwarizmi, who mixed numbers with unknowns and invented algebra, with its *abc*s, *x*s, and *y*s.

This Persian mathematician, astronomer, and geographer wanted a new math to use in problems dealing with farming, inheritance, and lawsuits. His innovative system was published in a book called *al-Kitāb al-mukhtasar fī Hisab al-Jabr wa-al-Muqabala* (The Compendious Book on Calculation by Completion and Balancing). Twelfth-century Latin translators changed the Arabic "al-jabr" (completion) into the "algebra" we know today.

Among many other books, al-Khwarizmi also wrote one that described Indian numbering systems using nine symbols and decimal notation. European translators called the book *Algoritmi de numero Indorum* (Al-Khwarizmi on Hindu Numbers). From that Latin version of his name comes the word "algorithm" —for a procedure or set of rules for problem solving. So what is *a*? A is for al-Khwarizmi, algebra, and algorithm!

Just sign your initials.

Book signing by Muhammad ibn Musa al-Khwarizmi

WILD ABOUT MATH

"THAT SOUNDS A LITTLE TOO MUCH like cheating. In fact, it all sounds like cheating...using math to help you do better in sports, art, and now music," said Mr. Lake. "I can't allow that!"

"Oh no, you mustn't," Ms. Norton said, tripping over a music stand as she rushed to speak up. "Numbers do nothing to nurture creativity or feed the soul, and self-expression can't be reduced to equations. Children should learn directly from life itself and experience the beauty of nature firsthand, not from a book or computer."

"If that's what you believe," said Sam, "you should take a closer look at nature. There's more math out there than you think."

"If it's out there, can we get out there, too?" asked the cameraman. "It's getting a little stuffy with all you people crowded in here."

"Why don't we go out to the new teaching garden by

the science room?" suggested the vice principal. That idea met with quite a few cheers, so we all trooped out to the area with the sunflowers, the butterfly-attracting plants, and all the other stuff the science teacher made us plant last spring.

You'd think the garden would have a calming effect, but the bees were making Ms. Norton even more agitated than usual. Or maybe just grouchier.

"Look around you! Where can you possibly find math out here?" she snapped. A bee zoomed directly in front of her and she gave a little shriek, backing into an anthill.

"Let's start with bees," said Sam, trying not to laugh. "Or ants. How do you think they know where to go?"

"Uh…Google Maps?" I said.

"Well, they do have a kind of 'anternet' to figure out *when* to go out," answered Sam. "Scientists at Stanford University discovered that harvester ant colonies decide how many ants to send out searching for food using an algorithm just like the Transmission Control Protocol (TCP) algorithm used to avoid congestion on the Internet."

"And look," said Sam, directing everyone's attention to a bee headed for our observation hive in the corner. "That bee estimates

HONEYBEES USE wall-to-wall tessellating hexagons to make storage cells for honey. Smart choice. Hexagons hold more honey and take less wax to build than triangles and squares. Less work too.

THE ANTS GO MARCHING EIGHT BY EIGHT—the little one stopped to navigate...wait, that's not how the song goes! Tunisian desert ants zigzag all over the place searching for food. As soon as they find something, they grab it and march straight back to the nest. They aren't following a scent or chemical trail—if they were, they would retrace the same zigzag path back. Instead, they're using "dead reckoning," constantly updating their distance and direction compared with where they began, and plotting a direct route back at each point. Sailors and pilots used dead reckoning to navigate the seas long before the Global Positioning System was invented, and Apollo astronauts used it on their moon missions. For humans, dead reckoning required doing arithmetic and trigonometry, step by step, with lots of help from charts, measuring tools, and, eventually, computers. Ants measure distance by counting their steps and, using the sun as a compass, instinctively calculate the most direct route for the long march home.

distance by processing how quickly images of trees and other markers move in its eyes as it flies past. Watch what happens when it gets back to the hive."

We made our way to the glassed-in hive. "Oh no," I groaned. "There's a tessellation in that honeycomb." Whoa. Did I really just say that? Sam had just succeeded in making me (me!) see math.

Sam grinned. "Here," he said, pointing as the bee flew into the plastic entry tube. "Let's see how far it's come."

"It looks like it's doing a little victory dance," said the reporter.

"You could call it that," Sam replied. "The dance tells the other bees there's pollen to collect, and encodes all the info they need to find it."

WHEN BUSY BEES can't stop to talk, body language helps!

CIRCLE DANCE

"Woohoo, food!" This simple circle means the pollen is close by —50 meters (164 feet) or less.

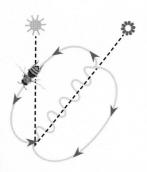

WAGGLE (FIGURE-EIGHT) DANCE

"Dinner's going to be a little late...and it's that-a-way."

The longer the bee waggles, the greater the distance to the pollen—1 second = about 3/4 km (1/2 mile).

The waggle up the middle is angled to show where the pollen is compared with the sun.

"You're telling us that these little insects can measure distance, time, and angles, and do all the calculations needed to chart a course for other bees to follow?" Ms. Norton was having a hard time with this. Mr. Lake too.

"Yes," Sam continued, "and it's not just insects that use math. An owl pinpoints its prey using triangulation—it figures out distances based on the triangle formed by its two ears and the tiny squeaks or rustles of its victim."

FETCH! One day, during a game of fetch at the beach, mathematics professor Timothy J. Pennings noticed that when he angled his throw into the water, his dog, Elvis, would streak partway down the sand before plunging in and swimming for the ball. Pennings realized that each time, his dog was working out how to get to the ball in the shortest amount of time, taking into account his faster running speed on the beach and slower swimming speed in the water. So, to figure out just how far to run before jumping in, Elvis was doing a calculus problem, just like the ones the professor assigned to his students! Trust a mathematician to notice!

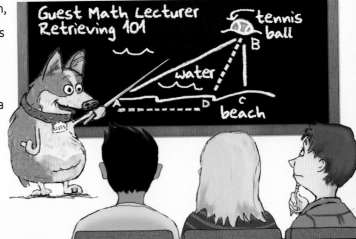

SOPHIE GERMAIN

(1776—1831)

SOPHIE GERMAIN'S PARENTS were shocked: their 13-year-old daughter insisted on studying mathematics! They took away her heat, candles, and clothes so she wouldn't study at night. It didn't work.

Why the fuss? Back in 18th-century Paris, serious math was for men. Women were banned from the new math and science academy. But Sophie, whose tutors wouldn't take her seriously, was determined. She sneaked lecture notes and submitted assignments to L'École Polytechnique as "Monsieur LeBlanc." But the professor—a famous mathematician named Legrange—wanted to meet his clearly brilliant student and soon her secret was out: he was a she!

Sophie's alter ego came in handy when she started writing to the great German mathematician Carl Gauss. But her cover was blown again when she asked her friend, a French general, to make sure Gauss wasn't killed when Napoleon's armies invaded Germany. Gauss was shocked to learn Sophie's true identity but admired the young woman's brilliance and determination. Who wouldn't? Today, a school, a hotel, a street in Paris, and a certain set of prime numbers are named after Sophie Germain—not "Monsieur LeBlanc"!

Pretty sure this is NOT good parenting!

Judging by their stubborn looks, it was clear Mr. Lake and Ms. Norton weren't buying it. Sam shrugged, but he was starting to look discouraged. "Call it evolution, or instinct if you want. It's still math, even if it's not the way we do math."

JEREMY WRESTLES WITH THE WEIRD STUFF

SO, IF A LOT OF THIS STUFF is instinct, are there any animals that do math the way we do? I don't mean badly (ha ha!) but, you know, can animals work with actual numbers, or at least with ideas like "more" or "less"? Sam says that chimpanzees' math comes the closest to ours: they understand fractions, can learn symbols for numbers, and can do easy adding and subtracting—kind of like your typical first-grader. Then there are the animals that do math more like your baby brother: trained rats estimate well enough to get treats by pressing a lever the right number of times. Lions "count" the number of roars they hear before deciding whether they should stand and fight or just run! And when shown two test tubes holding fruit flies (yum!), salamanders will choose the one holding more.

Fruit flies? Uh...are jellybeans an option?

Sam leaned over and whispered to me, "I guess it's hard to take, the idea of a bug being smarter than you are." Out loud he said, "Maybe we should try looking at something that doesn't involve calculations. Math that's just there."

FLOWER POWER

MS. NORTON RUSHED OVER to the flowerbeds and picked something up. "Math that's *just there*? What's just there is the beauty of nature. Look at the elegance of this creation," she exclaimed, holding a shiny, spiral-shaped shell. "You can't tell me this has anything to do with math."

"That shell," said Sam, "is a great example."

Ms. Norton didn't look pleased.

"This is the home of a mollusk called the chambered nautilus. At first, the space it lives in is smaller than a pea. But as the animal grows, it has to keep building new shell chambers. The cool thing is," said Sam, taking the shell from Ms. Norton and tracing the ridges with his finger, "it keeps exactly the same angle as it winds outward, creating a mathematical shape called a 'logarithmic spiral.'"

"What's so special about a logarithmic spiral?" I asked.

"It follows a strict mathematical rule: for every turn, the distance from the start is multiplied by the same amount," said Sam. "Got a piece of paper?" he asked, borrowing a pencil and a ruler from Ms. Kay.

I handed him a couple of sheets—my math homework, actually.

"This is a 'golden rectangle,'" he said as he sketched, "a special case of logarithmic spiral. If you measure the sides and take their ratio, you get a number called the 'golden ratio,' also known as *phi*. It's an

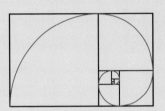

irrational number—remember those? Phi starts with 1.618...and never ends."

"Oh, right."

"And look," Sam continued, "if I divide this rectangle to get a square, the remaining rectangle is another golden rectangle. Keep doing this, and you get a smaller golden rectangle, and another, and another—you get the picture—and pretty soon you'll see a logarithmic spiral."

"Hey, I know all about this!" said Oscar importantly. "Leonardo da Vinci and other Renaissance artists thought golden rectangles—and other 'golden' shapes—made for perfect proportions for buildings and paintings. There are several golden rectangles in the *Mona Lisa*. The artist in me never thought of it as math, but the mathematician in me sees it now," he declared.

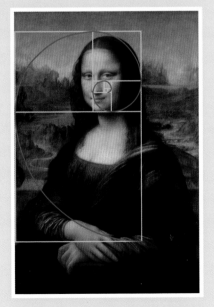

IS THE WORLD SPIRALING OUT OF CONTROL?

On many trees and plants, the leaves spiral up the stem as they grow so that each leaf is perfectly positioned for maximum sunlight.

A peregrine falcon's eyes are fixed to either side of its head. Diving in a logarithmic spiral lets it keep one eye on its prey *and* hold its head straight, for an aerodynamic chase.

Scientists aren't sure why, but insects approach lights in a logarithmic spiral of doom.

IMPORTANT:
No moths were injured during this re-enactment.

Galaxies like our Milky Way have spiral-shaped arms made of stars, gas, and dust.

Hurricanes swirl in a fast and logarithmic spiral as winds pulled in toward the low-pressure center are deflected by the Earth's spin.

"Enough with the rectangles and spirals!" cried Mr. Lake. "They're making me dizzy. I think I'm seeing spirals in those sunflowers!"

"That's because there *are* spirals in the sunflowers," said Sam with a grin. "Two groups of them, starting in the middle of the sunflower, one winding clockwise and the other counterclockwise. *And* the number of spirals in each direction is a perfect example of 'Fibonacci numbers.'"

"And what," asked Mr. Lake in a tired, tired voice, "are Fibonacci numbers? Or do I want to know?"

"They're numbers that follow a particular pattern discovered by Fibonacci, the mathematician who brought the idea of zero to Europe. Each new number comes from adding the two before. So 1, 1, 2, 3, 5, 8, 13, and so on."

FIBONACCI FRENZY! Fibonacci numbers turn up everywhere in nature. The number of petals on some flowers, the number of spirals formed by the scales on a pineapple or the seeds in a sunflower, the number of seed chambers in an apple or a cucumber—they're all Fibonacci numbers. You'll even find them on your dinner plate. Next time you have cauliflower for dinner, you can say you can't eat it because you have to count all the florets spiraling out from the center —it's your math homework!

At this point, Sam stopped and looked at Mr. Lake. "But you're right—time for a change."

Was that actually concern I was seeing on Sam's face? I took a look at Mr. Lake for myself—he *was* a little green. Maybe that's why Sam didn't go on about the Fibonacci numbers.

JEREMY WRESTLES WITH THE WEIRD STUFF

HERE'S SOMETHING REALLY WEIRD: Fibonacci numbers are linked to those logarithmic spirals we talked about earlier. Check this out. Go along the Fibonacci sequence and divide each number by the one before it, like this: $2 \div 1 = 2$, $3 \div 2 = 1.5$, $5 \div 3 = 1.666$, $8 \div 5 = 1.6$, $13 \div 8 = 1.625$. Keep going—the answers get closer and closer to the irrational number *phi*: 1.618...

Spooky...

As it turned out, Sam wasn't so concerned with Mr. Lake's condition. He was just eager to get on to something even more mind-bending.

"Now for the really wild stuff!" said Sam. "Fractals. You can see fractals all over nature."

Mr. Lake looked over at Ms. Norton and mouthed the word "fractal?" She just shrugged.

"The word fractal comes from Latin, and means 'fractured'—you know, broken." Sam pointed out a large plant. "See how each frond on this fern breaks down into smaller and smaller fronds? Or check out

that tree over there—see how the branches look like smaller trees?"

"I get it," said Emily. "Mountain ranges too—you can break them down into smaller and smaller jagged peaks, right down to the rocks. Or rivers—on a map you can see how the big ones split into small ones."

"So, a fractal is just the same shape getting smaller and smaller?" I asked.

"Yup. It's a never-ending pattern that repeats itself, no matter how far you zoom in or out...mathematicians call that 'self-similarity,'" answered Sam.

"That's nonsense—a branch can't go on forever," protested Mr. Lake.

"Not in nature," said Sam. "But geometric and algebraic fractals can go on as long as you like—it's one of the coolest things about them."

"I'll show you some examples," he added, pulling out his phone and doing a quick search. "Take a look at these."

HOLY FRACTAL DIMENSIONS, BATMAN! Did we land in some parallel realm, inhabited by fractal beings with fantastical properties? Fractals are real, even if they seem surreal—fractal shapes reproduce endlessly and exactly, at whatever scale.

Geometric fractals are made by simply repeating shapes. Koch snowflakes and Sierpinski triangles, for example, look orderly, just as you'd expect from a mathematical being.

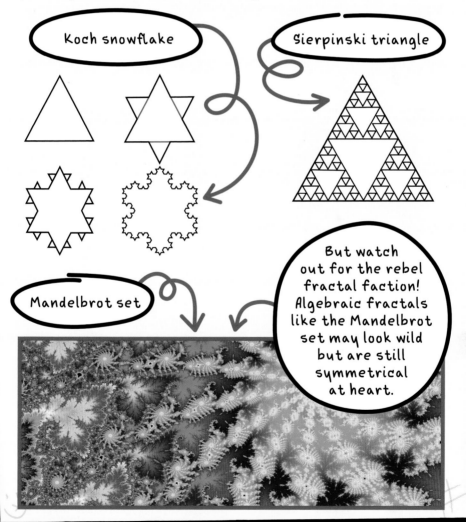

Koch snowflake

Sierpinski triangle

Mandelbrot set

But watch out for the rebel fractal faction! Algebraic fractals like the Mandelbrot set may look wild but are still symmetrical at heart.

"They're certainly very, uh, striking," admitted Ms. Norton, "but I don't see the point of studying pretty patterns."

"You'd be amazed," answered Sam. "Analyzing fractal patterns can help us create just about anything with a self-similar underlying structure. Fractals help us understand how parts of the human body work, how to make bridge cables stronger, and how to build tiny but powerful cellphone antennas. And because fractals are related to chaos theory, they can help us with unpredictable things like weather, earthquakes, and changes in the stock market!" Sam had to stop for a breath.

"It all sounds a little...complicated," Ms. Norton managed to fit in.

"It's not, though," said Sam. "Creating a fractal shape may look complicated, but all you do is repeat a shape or calculate an equation over and over again—it's called *iteration*. Remember we talked about how the computer-generated images in movies look so real? With computers, feeding each calculated result back into the same equation is easy, and the endless repetition of a simple rule actually ends up producing something that looks pretty irregular, and that makes it look more natural."

"Enough already!" said Ralph. "Don't take all those special effects apart—you're sucking all the fun out of them. I'll take my movie magic without the math."

ADA LOVELACE

(1815–1852)

ADA BYRON LOVELACE'S FATHER, the poet Lord Byron, was famously described as "mad, bad, and dangerous to know." When Ada's parents split up, her mother was determined to raise her with as much mathematics and science and as little contact with poets and literature as possible!

At the age of 12, Ada decided she wanted to fly. She studied birds, designed a horse-shaped flying machine powered by steam, and even wrote a book called *Flyology*.

When she was 17, one of Ada's tutors, noted mathematician Mary Somerville, introduced her to Charles Babbage, who was building a device that worked with numbers. However, it was Ada who saw the full potential of the "Analytical Engine," now considered a model for the modern computer. She recognized that because the machine could be programmed to translate numbers, it could do the same with other symbols, even musical notes.

The machine was never built, but Ada's published notes, including sample algorithms, were the the first to explain the concept of computer program-ming. There's even a programming language named after her.

TAKING SIDES

CONSIDER THIS A WARNING: Ralph is the class clown. He's always looking for a practical joke, and he thinks he's hilarious. Is he? Well... he once took an after-school comedy class, and the only comment the instructor gave was: "Ralph has his own brand of humor." Riiiiiight. And that brand is *corny*.

"The words 'fun' and 'math' don't exactly go together," said Ralph.

"Why not?" asked Sam. "Math can be fun, even funny."

"Are you for real?" asked one kid. I think he spoke for everybody.

"What did one math book say to the other?" asked Sam.

"Huh?"

"What did one math book say to the other?" he repeated patiently.

"Uh, I don't know," said Ralph.

"Leave me alone—I've got my own problems!"

"Hey, that's not bad! Got any more?" asked Ralph. "I can use them in my act!"

Oh no. Not the act! Everyone groaned. For his

JEREMY WRESTLES WITH THE WEIRD STUFF

IT DOESN'T MATTER IF YOU WIN OR LOSE—it's how you play the game. Sam's more logical than I am (and has way more patience) when it comes to thinking through the permutations in puzzles, like a Rubik's Cube. And he always wins at strategy games like checkers and chess. If I knew as much about probability as he does, I'd clean up in games of chance, too, like craps, roulette, or poker—not that we ever play those (hi, Mom)! I didn't need Sam to tell me that in Monopoly, the laws of probability mean plenty of chances to land in jail, but his tips on the next most-likely landing spots will definitely come in handy. I once told Sam that beating me might be easy but he'd never win against a computer. No way, he said; artificial intelligence easily wins games like chess by calculating ahead every possible move. But humans beat the pants off computers at games like Go, which need intuition to understand new scenarios. Well, now *he's* wrong! With human-like learning algorithms, computers finally defeated a professional Go champion for the first time, in October 2015.

> When it comes to fun and games, maybe Sam's got an unfair edge.

birthday, instead of just having some kids over to eat pizza and watch DVDs, Ralph puts on his own comedy show. We all like Ralph, but seriously? Most of his jokes are real groaners.

Sam laughed. "Okay, no more lame jokes. Maybe you can go with a circus-themed birthday this year, with some cool tricks. I can show you how to walk through a postcard."

Ralph's eyes lit up. "Yeah!"

Mr. Lake said nothing, but I could see "No. Way." written all over his face.

We followed Sam and Ralph back to the art room.

Sam found a small rectangular piece of heavy paper and started folding and snipping while we crowded around. When he was done, Sam unfolded the postcard into a huge loop and dropped it over Ralph's head. We all cheered.

"My act will be *sooo* good!" cried Ralph.

Mr. Lake tapped his foot impatiently. "Enough of this—we've strayed quite a bit from math—"

"Actually, we haven't," said Sam. "It's all geometry—the regular sort, officially known as Euclidean geometry—and fractals, topology…"

"Topo-what?" I asked.

"Topology—let *me* explain," said Ralph.

I looked at him skeptically. "*You* know what topology is?"

"Sure," said Ralph. "The mathematics of making my act top-notch!" He looked around, expecting a laugh. See what I mean about Ralph? Cor-ny.

"My turn," said Sam. "You might call topology a twisted take on the geometry we're used to."

"Like we don't have enough geometry?" I interrupted. "Why do we need another kind?"

"Sometimes," Sam explained, "mathematicians need to come up with new ideas when the old ones hold them back. Another name for topology is 'rubber-sheet geometry.' In plain old Euclidean geometry,

CHARLES LUTWIDGE DODGSON

(1832–1898)

QUEEN VICTORIA liked the book *Alice's Adventures in Wonderland* so much, she wanted more of the author's works. Surprise—most of his books were about math! Lewis Carroll, author of *Alice*, was actually mathematician Charles Lutwidge Dodgson.

Talk about a split personality! The seriously studious, stuttering mathematician lectured on logic and calculus at Oxford University, and wrote books with titles like *Condensation of Determinants*. On the other hand, he wasn't shy around children, and wrote nonsense poems, stories, and fairy letters (sometimes in looking-glass writing).

Deep down, his personalities weren't as different as they seemed. The common thread? Mathematics! He liked folding origami shapes and playing with tangrams (picture puzzles made using only seven shapes cut from a square). He invented word and math puzzles, and games such as Arithmetical Croquet, played on paper or in your head with numbers instead of mallets and hoops, and circular billiards, played on a round table with no pockets. Even his children's books are full of mathematics—the Mad Hatter in *Alice* uses this logic: "Why, you might as well say that 'I see what I eat' is the same thing as 'I eat what I see.'"

CHARLES LUTWIDGE DODGSON
SENSE

LEWIS CARROLL
NON–SENSE

TWISTED TRICKS

COME ONE, COME ALL! Step right up for the greatest show on earth! Prepare to be amazed by astonishing feats of mathematics!

1. **The Incredible Postcard Portal!** Math or no math, there's no way anybody can fit through a little 3 1/2- x 5-inch piece of cardboard...or can they?

   Don't be fooled by the small amount of space the postcard covers. With some fancy folding, this tiny area packs an incredibly long perimeter.

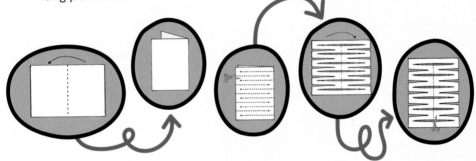

2. **The Amazing Shrinking Quarter!** Can you put a quarter through a dime-sized hole in a piece of paper?

   Think stretch instead of shrink. The diameter of the dime-sized circle may be too small, but the diameter of the oval you create by stretching the hole isn't.

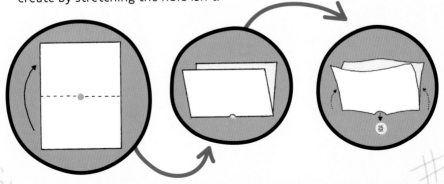

3. **The Impossible Topological Handcuff Escape!** Let's see you get out of this one (no amputation, please!):

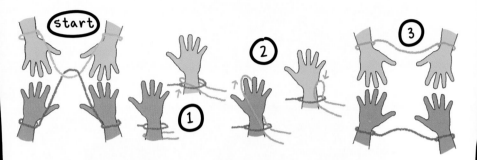

(1) Push the middle of your string under the loop on your partner's wrist, toward her fingers. (2) Loop it over her hand, back under the bit on her wrist, and (3) you're free.

4. **The Miraculous Traveling Knot!** Amaze your audience by tying a knot in a skipping rope without letting go of the ends. Just cross your arms first, then pick up an end in each hand. Uncross your arms to transfer the knot over to the rope.

shapes are rigid, and the same only if everything matches up exactly. When you're talking topology, it's a completely different story. Take a shape like a circle and really deform it—shrink it, stretch it, warp it any way you want. Even if it ends up looking like a square, you haven't changed it, not unless you've cut, pasted, or punched a hole in it."

The whole time he'd been talking, Sam had been busy cutting long strips of paper. I wondered why. After giving one of the strips a half-twist and taping the ends together, he handed the loop of paper to Ralph. "Here's another topology trick. This is called a Möbius strip.

Tell me if it's one-sided or two-sided."

"What?" asked Ralph.

"Draw a line down the middle of it. Keep going...now you're back where you started. Look!"

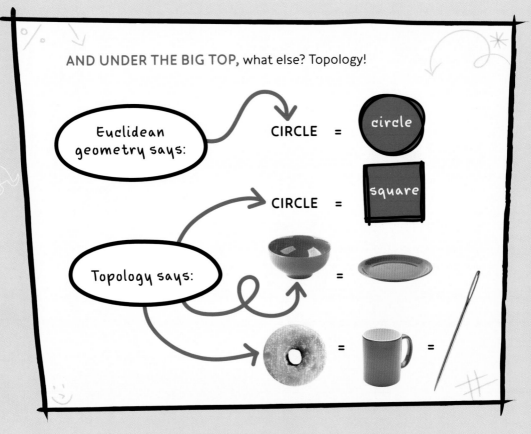

AND UNDER THE BIG TOP, what else? Topology!

Euclidean geometry says:

CIRCLE = circle

CIRCLE = square

Topology says:

=

=

=

"Weird!" cried Ralph. "How did I draw on both sides, when I never flipped the strip over?"

"Like I said, what's abnormal to us is perfectly normal to topologists," said Sam. "Surfaces, and inside and outside regions, and the way they're connected—that's what topologists look at."

"But why?" I asked.

DIY: ONE SIDE OR TWO?

WHOSE SIDE ARE YOU ON, ANYWAY? Topologists will tell you that a strip of paper has just one side, and will bend over backwards to prove it! It's a contortionist's delight—witness the wonderful world of Möbius strips.

1. Cut, twist, and tape:

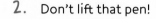

2. Don't lift that pen!

3. Now snip a hole in the strip and cut in half along the pencil line. Huh? One loop, not two?

MATHEMATICIAN FELIX KLEIN'S twist on the Möbius strip is a one-sided bottle. It exists only in the fourth dimension, but artists love creating 3-D versions—from knitted Klein bottle hats to Klein bottle-shaped playgrounds.

"Topology gives mathematicians new ways to think about problems—like what if the universe isn't infinite, but wraps around itself with no edges or boundaries, like a Möbius strip? Or, what's the best way to connect things like electrical circuits, computer networks, cell phone connections, and subway lines? Or, how do you simplify a maze so the way out is clear?"

Sam handed Ralph another loop, with three half-twists this time. "Now cut this one down the middle."

"That's so tangled," Ralph protested. "I'll get a knot!"

"Nothing wrong with knots," said Sam. "Looking at and unraveling

JEREMY WRESTLES WITH THE WEIRD STUFF

FINDING WALDO IS—WAS!—loads of fun. Back then (wayyy back), I took my time, sightseeing across the page, unlike Randal Olson. The artificial intelligence researcher mapped out Waldo's whereabouts from seven *Where's Waldo* books, and figured out where Waldo's never (or almost never) at. But never mind where he isn't—where *is* he? The fastest way to check every possible location without backtracking was to use a genetic algorithm, which mixes the best of a bunch of possible solutions to produce new solutions, randomly messes with a few of these to get variety, then does it all over again with the best from this new group, and so on. In this way, the algorithm tirelessly fiddles with the answer, making a good solution better, until finally, a keeper! The answer? Not telling.

Quick, where's Waldo?

messy mathematical knots can help scientists explain a lot, including how DNA winds and unwinds, and maybe even how the entire universe works. Scientists are seriously thinking that 'superstring theory' might explain it all. This Theory of Everything—I'm not kidding about the name—says the universe is made of tiny, 1-dimensional strings vibrating in a 10- or 11-dimensional world."

I know 1-D is a line, 2-D is a square, 3-D is a cube, 4-D is a hypercube...but what does a 10-D world look like? This was mind-blowing stuff. I was glad when Ralph interrupted my thoughts!

"Hey, was I right or what?" Ralph said, holding up the loop he had cut, which was now in a knot.

"So you like these tricks?" asked Sam.

"Sure," answered Ralph. "What's *knot* to like?"

We all groaned, even Sam. But not Mr. Lake.

"Fun and games is fine for some folks," he said, obviously still looking for reasons to back up his ban. "But math isn't just fun and games and those Fibo-fractal-phi things. It's full of all those complicated calculations and numbers—far too many numbers."

That's when the reporter spoke up. "Mr. Lake," she said, "clearly, you are not convinced. However, I'd like to hear from the kids."

She quickly turned to me. "You weren't too upset with the math ban earlier. What do you think now?" she demanded.

CRIMES AND PRIMES

WHAT DID I THINK about math now? What could I say? Sam was my friend, but…well…something was still bothering me.

"Sure, this stuff is pretty cool, but…well, numbers themselves *are* kind of boring," I admitted. Did I just agree with Lake? I was so lame!

"You're right!" exclaimed Natasha. "Numbers are just *blah*. 1, 2, 3, 4…1 plus 1 equals 2, 2 times 3 equals 6. No surprises, no mystery."

No surprises there either. Natasha is so into mystery novels, she actually believes she's in one. She's always looking for ulterior motives and asking nosy questions.

Sam looked really surprised, and more than a bit frustrated. "Boring?" he said, his voice rising. "No mystery? What about numbers like prime numbers?"

"*Bor*-ing. What's so interesting about them? 'A prime number is a whole number bigger than one that can't be divided without a remainder by any number except itself and one.'" Natasha rattled off the definition we all had to memorize last year.

DIY: PRIME TIME!

YOU WANT A SMALL PRIME NUMBER? No biggie.

To find small prime numbers, use the Sieve of Eratosthenes, an ancient algorithm:

1. Write out all the numbers from 2 to, say, 30 (skip 1, it's definitely not a prime number).

    2 3 4 5 6 7 8 9 10 11 12 13
    14 15 16 17 18 19 20 21 22
    23 24 25 26 27 28 29 30

2. Find the smallest number (2) and cross out its multiples.

    2 3 ~~4~~ 5 ~~6~~ 7 ~~8~~ 9 ~~10~~ 11 ~~12~~ 13
    ~~14~~ 15 ~~16~~ 17 ~~18~~ 19 ~~20~~ 21 ~~22~~
    23 ~~24~~ 25 ~~26~~ 27 ~~28~~ 29 ~~30~~

3. Find the next smallest number (3), and cross out its multiples. Keep repeating with the next smallest number until you can't cross out any more.

    2 3 ~~4~~ 5 ~~6~~ 7 ~~8~~ ~~9~~ ~~10~~ 11 ~~12~~ 13
    ~~14~~ ~~15~~ ~~16~~ 17 ~~18~~ 19 ~~20~~ ~~21~~ ~~22~~
    23 ~~24~~ ~~25~~ ~~26~~ ~~27~~ ~~28~~ 29 ~~30~~

4. *Ta da!* The remaining numbers are primes.

"They're interesting enough to be worth money," said Sam. That got our attention.

"How much?" asked Natasha.

"A LOT."

"What? Why?" Natasha was skeptical.

JEREMY WRESTLES WITH THE WEIRD STUFF

DESPERATE FOR PATTERNS, any patterns at all, in prime numbers? This is as close as it gets...

→ **Absolute prime:** a prime number that stays prime, no matter how you arrange it (e.g., 337, 373, 733)

→ **Circular prime:** a prime number that stays prime when you move each digit to the back of the line (e.g., 1,193, 1,931, 9,311, 3,119)

→ **Holey prime:** a prime number made up only of digits with holes (e.g., 89)

→ **Unholey prime:** a prime number made up of digits without holes, duh! (e.g., 1,117)

→ **Emirp:** a prime even when reversed (e.g., 13 or 1,061)

→ **Bemirp (bidirectional emirp):** a prime that reverses to give a prime and still gives primes when both are flipped upside down (e.g., 1,061 reversed is 1,601; flipped, they give 1,901 and 1,091)

Unholey prime? Emirp? Mathematicians can be as corny as Ralph!

"When it comes to big prime numbers," Sam answered, "making sure a number is divisible only by one and itself is a huge mathematical job. That's why $150,000 is waiting for the first person to find a 100-million-digit prime number. The biggest so far is 22,338,618 digits long. There's also a $250,000 prize for the first billion-digit prime number."

"Nice!" said Ralph. "Who's putting up all that cash?"

"It's a group that wants ordinary people chipping in computer time to solve massive problems," said Sam. "It takes a lot of computers running 24/7 to find prime numbers. The bigger the prime, the more useful it is for making secret codes."

"What do you mean?" asked Natasha, instantly alert.

THERE'S SAFETY IN NUMBERS! If you want to stump Internet hackers or credit card scammers—maybe even spies—use two huge prime numbers to create your code keys. That's what RSA encryption, widely used for protecting online credit-card transactions and email, does. Multiply the primes together to get a semi-prime number for further calculations to keep your cyber secrets safe. Breaking the decryption code means figuring out which two primes were used, and that's not easy! Most Internet companies use 2,048-bit or even 4,096-bit keys. Factoring a 768-bit (232-digit) semi-prime took hundreds of computers two years to factor, so we're safe...for now. The game-changer: quantum computers, based on the physics of really, really small particles, will process information incredibly fast but aren't quite ready for use yet.

Aha! Sam was shrewd—he'd tapped into Natasha's fixation with mysteries.

"Secret codes and quantum computers?" exclaimed Mr. Lake. "We're not living in some thriller espionage novel. This is the real world. And we have real problems, right here in our own neighborhood. I'd like to see your fancy math ideas help with that!"

"Do you mean all those burglaries we've had in the last few months?" Natasha asked. "My aunt thought they'd figured it out at one point. The intruder's pretty clumsy, and left traces of blood at a couple of houses." Natasha's aunt is our town's police chief.

"DNA evidence, right?" I interrupted. "What happened? That always closes the case on TV!"

JEREMY WRESTLES WITH THE WEIRD STUFF

CAN CRIME PATTERNS solve cases of stolen glory? Four hundred and fifty years ago, French mathematician Blaise Pascal used a mathematical stack of numbers to answer a friend's gambling question. The origins of the triangle he used go back farther, to Indian, Chinese, and Persian scholars. And European mathematicians worked on it, too. But guess who got naming rights? We know it as Pascal's triangle, but you can rightfully call it Tartaglia's triangle in Italy, the Khayyam triangle in Iran, or Yang Hui's triangle in China.

Check out page 87 to see me—yes, me!—explain some of Pascal's triangle.

ELEVEN-YEAR OLD ENTREPRENEUR Mira Modi has a business providing secure passwords. She rolls six-sided dice to get random numbers, then matches the numbers to a list of words, generating easy-to-remember, nonsensical sentences with the words.

"It's not that simple, Sherlock," said Natasha. "All that DNA testing shows is whether the blood found at the scene and blood from the suspect has the same DNA code in parts—specifically, 13 pairs of genes that are the most different from person to person. The probability of the samples from two people matching like that is one in trillions (not counting identical twins), according to many experts, so you'd think a match means certain guilt! But the method isn't perfect—contaminated or damaged sample DNA can mess up the results; and it doesn't take into account alibi, motive, or other circumstances."

"And don't forget," added Sam, "that you need to understand how probability works, too."

"So since the DNA results were inconclusive, my aunt's sending in extra cops to patrol the area…it's a 'hot spot'—you know, like the maps you see on the detective shows all covered in pins?" said Natasha.

"Or what you get when you type 'pizza' into Google Maps!" I joked.

"Yeah, something like that. Patterns showing hot spots and clusters for recent burglaries, car thefts, or gang violence can tell cops tons of crime-preventive stuff—like where gang territories start and end, what locations attract the most crime and why, and whether extra policing will shut down crime or just push it somewhere else," Natasha continued. "My aunt now thinks it's the same guy committing all the

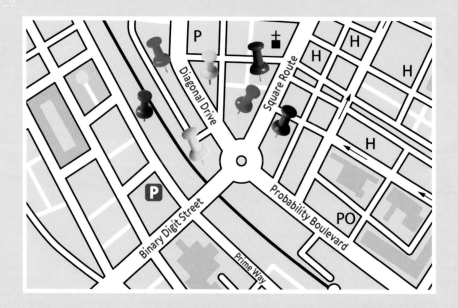

robberies, so she's meeting with some people at the university about something called geographic profiling, which is really useful for serial crime."

"Hey, I heard about that," said Sam. "They've got mathematicians looking for patterns in the robbery locations. In serial crime cases, these patterns can't predict a serial offender's next move, but they might point to where the culprit lives or works. The algorithm calculates the probability based on patterns in the way the culprit moves around and where he or she chooses to go."

MATHEMATICIAN CARL GAUSS foiled his teacher's time-wasting schemes at the age of 10: asked to add the numbers from 1 to 100, he arranged them in 50 pairs, each totaling 101 (100 + 1, 99 + 2, etc.). Multiplying 101 x 50, he had the answer in seconds!

SRINIVASA RAMANUJAN

(1887–1920)

FOR MOST MATHEMATICIANS, life's probably not all about numbers. But try telling that to Srinivasa Ramanujan. Growing up in India, his obsession started early: he taught himself mathematics from an old book until he could go to college on a scholarship. But his sole interest was mathematics—he failed everything else. As a dropout, he could only find work as an accounts clerk.

He wrote to English mathematician G. E. Hardy for help. Hardy thought it was a scam, but something about Ramanujan's long, messy list of unproved theorems intrigued him, and he ended up inviting Ramanujan to Cambridge to work. Once he got to England, Ramanujan suffered from the cold weather. And food shortages brought on by World War I made it hard for the vegetarian mathematician to eat properly—plus he often forgot to eat. But as Ramanujan grew weaker, his number fixation grew stronger. When he was hospitalized, Hardy visited him and, looking for a subject of conversation, commented that his taxi's number—1,729—was a dull one. Ramanujan—tired and frail—immediately defended 1,729 as the smallest number that could be expressed as the sum of two cubes in two different ways ($10^3 + 9^3$ or $12^3 + 1^3$). Ramanujan returned to India and died shortly after, at age 33.

$$885,623,890,831 = 7,511^3 + 7,730^3$$
$$= 8,759^3 + 5,978^3$$
$$= 3,943 \times 14,737 \times 15,241$$

"Right," said Natasha. "Displayed on a map, the possibilities are narrowed down in a big way for the police."

The bell rang—lunch hour was over. Sam looked at Mr. Lake. So did everyone else. "Well, sir, what do you think now?"

JEREMY WRESTLES WITH THE WEIRD STUFF

HE LURKS IN THE SHADOWS, waiting, watching...bingo! A likely victim wanders into view, young, alone, unaware. He bides his time and, then, when darkness falls, ambush!

For a minute there, I thought I was trapped in a bad slasher film! But no, we're talking about a real predator on the prowl. Geographic profiling showed marine researchers that the great white shark selects and kills a seal in ways eerily like the way a serial killer stalks and murders his or her victim: both have an MO—modus operandi—a base of operations, and a premeditated plan of attack. (Cut Jaws some slack, though—a shark's gotta eat.) Criminologists are working with biologists to recruit sharks, bats, bees, lions, and other creatures as crime-busting sidekicks. Humans are just mammals on the move, after all, and the mathematics of geographic profiling applies to us all—what they learn about bats helps to catch the baddies.

Hey, who gets to be Batman, and who's Robin?

THE AFTER-MATH

THIS WAS IT. Sam had done his best, but was it good enough? It was up to Mr. Lake to decide if math would stay or math would go. Believe it or not, I now completely agreed with Sam. Math *is* important and exciting and a part of everything we do. And, turns out it's actually kind of fun! It might have taken me a while to come around, but hey, I'm not an easy guy to convince. I'm pretty sure all the kids, even Oscar, were on side now, too. How could Mr. Lake *not* agree?

"This has been a very entertaining hour," said the director slowly, "but I'm not changing my mind. The ban stays."

What?

Mr. Lake's face turned red as he tried to make himself heard over all the kids talking at once. "Math is still too much work, and much too complicated for you children, no matter how useful it might seem! I have your best interests at heart. You'll thank me one day!" he shouted.

Through all this, Sam stayed quiet. "Well, I guess I haven't convinced you," he finally said. "So, like I promised, I will work for you after school, starting today if you like. But could I have an advance on my first 30 days' pay?"

That was it? Sam was just giving up? I looked around at the teachers for help—Ms. Kay didn't make a move. Neither did the vice principal. We were out of luck. Mr. Lake nodded, that smirky smile on his face again. "Why, of course, Sam." Yeah, he was in a good mood *now*.

"Thanks, Mr. Lake," Sam replied. "I'll just calculate it out."

He walked over to the flip chart where Oscar had done his sketch, flipped to a clean page, and drew this table:

DAY	PAY FOR THE DAY	TOTAL PAY
1	0.01	0.01
2	0.02	0.03
3	0.04	0.07
4	0.08	0.15
5	0.16	0.31

"No way," exclaimed Ralph. "After five days of work, Sam's going to make only *31 cents*? That's not fair!"

Sam kept writing.

DAY	PAY FOR THE DAY	TOTAL PAY
6	0.32	0.63
7	0.64	1.27
8	1.28	2.55
9	2.56	5.11
10	5.12	10.23
11	10.24	20.47
12	20.48	40.95
13	40.96	81.91
14	81.92	163.83
15	163.84	327.67
16	327.68	655.35

"Whoa," said Natasha. "Sam's going to make over $600 by the middle of the month. That's big money."

Ms. Norton was frowning as she watched the numbers grow. And then I saw it—genius! Mr. Lake saw it too—he got more and more fidgety with each line Sam wrote.

EXPONENTIAL GROWTH—what Sam is showing here—is a feature of a fable about grains of wheat (or rice) on a chessboard that was first recorded around 1000 CE by the Persian poet Ferdowsi.

DAY	PAY FOR THE DAY	TOTAL PAY
17	655.36	1,310.71
18	1,310.72	2,621.43
19	2,621.44	5,242.87
20	5,242.88	10,485.75
21	10,485.76	20,971.51
22	20,971.52	41,943.03
23	41,943.04	83,886.07
24	83,886.08	167,772.15
25	167,772.16	335,544.31
26	335,544.32	671,088.63
27	671,088.64	1,342,177.27
28	1,342,177.28	2,684,354.55
29	2,684,354.56	5,368,709.11
30	5,368,709.12	10,737,418.23

Mr. Lake's smile was gone now, and when Sam turned to give him the grand total for the month—nearly *11 million dollars*!—the director was sweating like mad.

"I've been thinking it over while you were doing your, er, calculations," said Mr. Lake.

Got him!

"And perhaps I was a bit hasty in making my decision," he continued. Warming up, he went on. "A little hard work doesn't hurt anybody, and math can be useful, no matter what other people say... yes, yes, I've always thought so, underneath it all. I'll admit math isn't my best subject—"

No kidding!

"—so I'd still like you to consider that after-school job, helping me brush up on my math skills." Mr. Lake smiled at Sam. He quickly added, "We'd have to negotiate a new wage, of course."

• • •

SO THE MATH PROGRAM stayed on the curriculum. Ms. Kay started a math club, which is pretty popular. Sam and I, Emily, Oscar, Jen, Ralph, Natasha, and some other kids joined. Even Ms. Norton came in to help! You wouldn't believe the stuff we got into: mazes and puzzles, higher dimensions, knot theory, logic and paradoxes, calculus, statistics, game theory, geometries I never even knew existed, and tons more.

We've all got big plans.

Emily's thinking biomechanics. Math will be her secret weapon. She likes how you can mathematically analyze something like a figure-skating jump or golf swing, and find out exactly what's needed to do it better. Or she'll calculate more energy-efficient or aerodynamic ways to help her win a race. Maybe even design a program that helps her work out just enough to improve, but not overdo it. A way to win without working too hard? There's got to be a way for me to use that!

Oscar thinks virtual reality is the way to go—forget just seeing and hearing, he wants the whole experience. He wants to build games with virtual worlds real enough for people to lose themselves in. The way he sees it, his artistic ideas will be so advanced he'll have to master the math himself—no problem for a genius like him. Or he could be a consultant for *The Simpsons*. (Don't tell me you didn't know about the hidden math! In one episode, Homer seems to have found a solution to the famously unsolvable equation of Fermat's Last Theorem!) Sure, they've had producers and writers who were mathematicians before,

but Oscar says, with him on board, the ratings will be unbeatable.

Jen wants to keep her band going. I don't always get her inspiration—she'll convert some mathematical concept like pi into MIDI notes and play them—but when Jen wants to do something, she usually does it, and does it well, so I won't be surprised to see her topping the charts one day. She also told Oscar to call her up if he ever needs a composer for his games, because she's keen on experimenting with all sorts of digital sound.

Ralph's holding on to his dream of becoming a super-celebrity. I'm not sure about that, but his act is better now. His jokes don't stink, his tricks are passable, and he's not too bad at juggling, actually. Maybe studying siteswap notation, which looks at juggling patterns in a mathematical way, helped. He's been thinking about robotics, too, ever since he heard that researchers are working on developing a robot that can juggle.

Natasha says she wants to be a cryptographer or cryptanalyst, you know, a code-maker or code-breaker. Spy stuff...yeah...I like the sound of that, too. If not, she might get into law enforcement—she's got this hunch that geographic profiling's the way to go.

Sam and me? Well, Sam says he's wanted to be a physicist since he was five. He wants to answer the big questions: What's time? What does space look like? How did the universe begin? The kind of mind-benders only math can answer.

As for me…I'll be the best friend of the guy who finally settles the Theory of Everything question. Other than that, hmmm…Ms. Kay thinks I'd make a great math teacher. I'm turning into a pro already, translating for Sam whenever he gets carried away. I show kids the cool side of math, using a lot of the examples Sam did. And when some new kid starts complaining that math is too hard, or that it's only for geniuses or geeks—when that happens, I tell them the story of the Great Number Rumble. And you know what they always end up saying?

That's math? Wow—go figure!

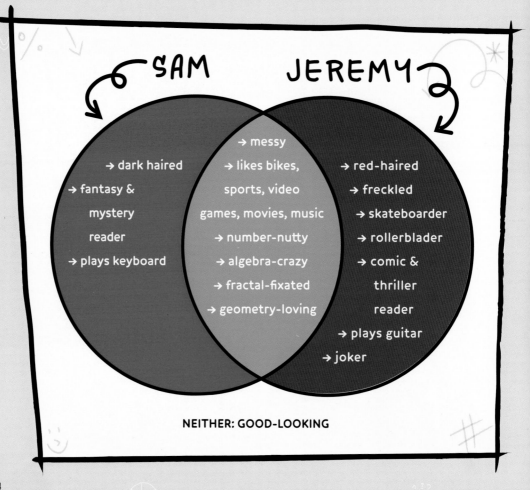

SAM

→ dark haired

→ fantasy & mystery reader

→ plays keyboard

→ messy

→ likes bikes, sports, video games, movies, music

→ number-nutty

→ algebra-crazy

→ fractal-fixated

→ geometry-loving

JEREMY

→ red-haired

→ freckled

→ skateboarder

→ rollerblader

→ comic & thriller reader

→ plays guitar

→ joker

NEITHER: GOOD-LOOKING

ALAN TURING

(1912–1954)

ALAN TURING, the father of artificial intelligence, was fascinated with the idea that computers could think, but insisted on proof. So he threw down a challenge: could a computer pass the "Turing test"? His test, also known as "the imitation game," was based on the idea that if a computer *was* intelligent, then we wouldn't be able to tell it apart from a real person. In the modern test, words appear onscreen, and humans have to decide if it's a human or computer talking. If they can't tell, the computer has passed the test.

Eccentric, witty, a bit of a slob, and a good long-distance runner, Turing was a brilliant math student. In his 20s, he was already planning the Turing machine, an early model of a general-purpose computer. During World War II, he was recruited to Britain's Bletchley Park, where talented mathematicians, cryptanalysts, and others worked to break German Enigma codes that were baffling the Allied forces. After the war, Turing worked on developing the first stored-program computers, artificial intelligence, and even an early computer chess program. He also studied mathematically formed patterns in animal coats and Fibonacci numbers in plant structures.

And while you pass a reverse Turing test (designed to confirm that the user is human) every time you fill out a CAPTCHA box on the Internet, so far no machine has ever passed the Turing test.

This guy's my hero!

SOLVING THE UNSOLVABLE PUZZLE!

TEN-YEAR-OLD ANDREW WILES loved math problems and got hooked on the ultimate mystery: Fermat's Last Theorem, which had remained unsolvable for centuries.

Fermat was a 17th-century mathematician who left a mysterious note in the margin of a book saying that the equation $x^n + y^n = z^n$ had no solutions when "n" is bigger than 2. He could prove it, too, the note claimed—except the margin was too small for his proof. Fermat died 28 years later without ever writing down this proof—talk about not getting your homework done! Mathematicians couldn't resist the challenge: if Fermat could prove it, so could they. Wrong! But working on it helped them solve a lot of other mathematical problems.

Wiles worked on the problem throughout his early teens, but got nowhere. He put the mystery aside, but a new, related problem gave him some fresh ideas. In 1993 came the sensational news: after seven years of secret research, Andrew Wiles had proved Fermat's Last Theorem! Mathematicians found an error, however, and Wiles spent another year checking his work. But inspiration struck again, and this time he really had solved the unsolvable! Fermat was right—when "n" is bigger than 2, the equation $x^n + y^n = z^n$ has no solutions.

KEEP CALM AND FIGURE ON

That's right, me!

JEREMY WRESTLES WITH PASCAL'S TRIANGLE

The first row is row zero. The second row is row 1. Yeah, weird, I know.

Add across rows for powers of 2
$2^1 = 2 = 1 + 1$
$2^2 = 4 = 1 + 2 + 1$
$2^3 = 8 = 1 + 3 + 3 + 1$
Exponential growth, like Sam's pay!

Every number is the sum of the numbers above it.
$5 = 1 + 4$

```
                1
              1   1
            1   2   1
          1   3   3   1
        1   4   6   4   1
      1   5  10  10   5   1
    1   6  15  20  15   6   1
  1   7  21  35  35  21   7   1
```

Look for Fibonacci numbers, powers of 11, and other patterns. And check it out—coloring the odd squares and leaving the even squares white gets you a Sierpinski triangle!

Forget Gauss's trick for adding numbers in a row. You can do it with this hockey stick pivot:
$1 + 2 + 3 + 4 = 10$

Keep adding rows... Pascal's triangle can go on forever!

GLOSSARY

Absolute prime: A prime number that stays prime, no matter how you arrange it (e.g., 337, 373, 733).

Algebra: A type of mathematics using letters and other symbols to represent numbers in equations.

Algorithm: A set of mathematical rules followed step by step to solve a problem.

Arc: A part of the way around a circle.

Arithmetic: The branch of mathematics dealing with calculations such as the addition, subtraction, multiplication, and division of numbers.

Bemirp (bidirectional emirp): A prime that reverses to give a prime and still gives primes when both are flipped upside down (e.g., 1,061 reversed is 1,601; flipped, they give 1,901 and 1,091).

Biomechanics: Science that analyzes movement in living systems and looks at the forces that act upon them.

Butterfly effect: A famous idea in chaos theory that describes how tiny disturbances can cause dramatic changes in complicated situations over time.

Calculus: The name for two types of mathematics—integral calculus and differential calculus. Integral calculus is one way of computing areas and volumes of complicated shapes. Differential calculus computes values that are always changing, such as how fast you're traveling on a trip where the car's speed keeps changing.

Catenary: A curve created from a heavy cord or chain that hangs between its two ends.

CGI (computer generated imagery): Three-dimensional images created using specialized computer software for film or special effects.

Chaos: Describes a situation that's always changing in an irregular way. What happens depends upon fixed rules but is unpredictable because the situation can change dramatically over a long period of time under the influence of small changes to conditions at the start.

Circular prime: A prime number that stays prime when you move each digit to the back of the line (e.g., 1,193; 1,931; 9,311; 3,119).

Combination: A selection made from a group of objects when the order of arrangement doesn't matter. *See also* Permutation.

Cryptanalyst: Somebody who deciphers the combination of symbols, letters, or numbers that make up a secret code; a code-breaker.

Cryptographer: Somebody who creates codes by combining symbols, letters, or numbers to hide information; a code-maker.

Dead reckoning: A method of figuring out the position of a ship or airplane that is moving only in straight lines and making sharp turns. The distance traveled between changes of direction can be calculated as long as time, speed, and direction can be measured.

Decimal: Describes numbers written in a base-10 system, in which each digit is 10 times higher than the one to its right; a decimal fraction is a non-whole-number written with a decimal point.

Diameter: The length of any line that cuts a shape such as a circle or ellipse exactly in half.

Dimension: A way of talking about the kind of space something takes up. A line has 1 dimension (1-D): length. A square has two dimensions (2-D): length and width. A cube has 3 dimensions (3-D): length, width, and height. Mathematicians think the universe could have 10 or more dimensions.

Emirp: A number that remains prime even when reversed (e.g., 13 or 1,061).

Estimate: To carefully guess or give an approximate value based on known information.

Exponential growth: An increase that starts out slow but grows faster as the total amount gets bigger.

Fermat's Last Theorem: A famous mathematical statement that says that no solutions exist for the equation $x^n + y^n = z^n$ if n is bigger than 2 and x, y, z are integers bigger than 0. Named for mathematician Pierre Fermat (1601–1665).

Fibonacci numbers: A sequence of numbers (e.g., 1, 1, 2, 3, 5, 8, 13, 21, 34) in which each number is formed by adding the two previous numbers. Named for mathematician Fibonacci (1170–1250).

Fractal: A mathematically constructed, never-ending pattern of shapes that are miniature versions of the whole shape. An algebraic fractal is made by calculating an equation repeatedly. A geometric fractal is made by repeating the same rule for changing a shape again and again.

Game Theory: A branch of mathematics that analyzes games, such as those played for fun, and looks at strategy and decision making in areas such as politics, economics, and the military.

Genetic algorithm: A problem-solving procedure that mixes the best of a group of possible solutions to produce new solutions, randomly makes changes to a few of these to get variety, and then repeats the process with the best from the new group until the ideal solution is found.

Geodesic dome: A framework of triangles or polygons.

Geometry: A branch of mathematics dealing with objects in space. Euclidean geometry deals with flat and solid (three-dimensional) shapes and is named after the mathematician Euclid (325–265 BCE), who laid out the basic theorems and rules of geometry. Non-Euclidean geometries deal with curved space.

Golden ratio: A ratio equal to approximately 1.618... (an irrational number), often appearing in nature. Also known as the golden section or phi (Φ).

Golden rectangle: a rectangle that has sides in the ratio 1:1.618.

Hexagon: A flat figure with six sides and six angles. A regular hexagon has six equal sides and six equal angles.

Holey prime: A prime number made up only of digits with holes (e.g., 89).

Hypercube: A four-dimensional object. Also called a tesseract.

Imaginary numbers: Numbers written as real numbers times i, which is the square root of -1 ($\sqrt{-1}$). i was invented to find the square roots of negative numbers, which is logically impossible with real numbers. *See also* Real numbers.

Infinity (∞): Endlessness. Numbers are infinite, i.e., there is always another number after the biggest number you can think of.

Integers: All whole numbers and negative numbers (e.g., -3, -2, -1, 0, 1, 2, 3).

Irrational numbers: Numbers that cannot be completely expressed as a ratio or decimal. They never end and never repeat in a logical pattern (e.g., pi or $\sqrt{2}$).

Iteration: The recycling of results back into the same equation or rule.

Klein bottle: A closed surface with no inside or outside, formed by passing one end of a tube through its side and joining it to the other end.

Knot: A mathematical knot is a closed curve, with no loose ends, in three-dimensional space.

Logarithmic spiral: An open-ended curve that coils around a given point without changing the angle of the curve. A three-dimensional spiral is known as a helix.

MIDI (musical instrument digital interface): A standardized method of communication that allows electronic musical instruments and computers to understand the same data.

Möbius strip: A one-sided object in topology that can be modeled by giving a strip of paper a half-twist before taping the ends together.

Motif: The basic unit in a repeated pattern.

Natural numbers: The set of the ordinary counting numbers (e.g., 1, 2, 3).

Origami: The art of folding paper.

Palindromes: Numbers, words, or phrases that read the same forwards or backwards. Examples of number palindromes are 121 and 34,743. Word palindromes include "madam" and "radar."

Parabola: The mathematical curve traced by a stream of water from a hose as it shoots up, curves near the top, and heads back down; or the path of a thrown ball.

Paradox: A statement or reasoning that leads to an impossible or obviously wrong solution. A famous example is Zeno's paradox. Zeno argued that if Achilles gives a tortoise a head start in a race, then Achilles will never catch up. Why? As soon as Achilles reaches the point where the tortoise was, the tortoise will have moved on to another point. The two racers will never be in the same place because the distance, no matter how short, can always be subdivided, and Achilles will always be trying to make up that infinitely small distance. In reality, time can't be divided infinitely, and the sum of infinitely many parts does not total an infinitely large number.

Parallel lines: Lines that will never meet because they are always the same distance apart.

Pascal's triangle: A triangular arrangement of numbers in which every number is the sum of the two numbers above it. The triangle is named after 17th-century French mathematician Blaise Pascal (1623–1662) but was recorded by a Chinese mathematician around 1300 CE and known earlier by Hindu and Arab scholars.

Pattern: A shape, design, or arrangement of numbers (or letters) that repeat in a regular way.

Percentage: An amount expressed as a fraction where the denominator is 100.

Perfect number: A number that equals the sum of its factors, not including itself. Six is a perfect number: $1 + 2 + 3 = 6$ and $1 \times 2 \times 3 = 6$.

Perimeter: The distance around a closed figure, e.g., a square or pentagon.

Permutation: A selection made from a group of objects, when the order of arrangement matters. *See also* Combination.

Perspective: The science of drawing on a two-dimensional surface to create the illusion of three dimensions.

Phi (φ): *See* Golden ratio.

Pi (π): An irrational number that is the ratio of the circumference of a circle to its diameter. It is usually shown as 3.142 but has been calculated to over a trillion decimal places.

Prime numbers: Any number greater than 1 with only two factors—1 and itself.

Probability: A branch of mathematics that uses numbers to predict how likely something is to happen.

Projective geometry: A type of geometry that studies the relationship between figures and their images, when projected onto a different surface (e.g., when a 3-D object is drawn realistically on paper).

Pythagorean theorem ($a^2 + b^2 = c^2$): The rule that states that the sum of the squares of two sides of a right-angled triangle is equal to the square of the hypotenuse (the longest side, which is opposite to the right angle).

Random-number generator: A device that produces numbers fairly, with no particular order or preference, e.g., dice, spinners, specially designed computer programs.

Ratio: A way of comparing two numbers (e.g., 2:1 or 2/1 or 2 to 1). Special ratios include pi and the golden ratio.

Rational numbers: Numbers that can be written as a ratio of whole numbers (fractions) or decimals (e.g., 0.25 or ½).

Real numbers: All rational and irrational numbers.

Self-similar: Having the same appearance at any magnification.

Semi-prime number: A number resulting from multiplying two prime numbers.

Sieve of Eratosthenes: A way of finding prime numbers that was invented by the Greek mathematician Eratosthenes (c. 230 BCE).

Siteswap notation: A way of writing down juggling patterns.

Square numbers: The product of a number multiplied by itself (e.g., $4 = 2 \times 2$—or 2 squared or 2^2). Also the number of evenly spaced dots needed to make a square.

Square roots: The number that is multiplied by itself to produce the square number (e.g., 3 is the square root of 9 because $3 \times 3 = 9$).

Statistics: The branch of mathematics that collects, analyzes, and interprets numerical facts.

Superstring theory: An idea that explains how the universe is made of tiny, 1-dimensional strings vibrating in a 10—or 11-dimensional world.

Surface area: The total amount of space covered by the outside of a 3-D object.

Tangram: A geometrical puzzle of Chinese origin, consisting of a square cut into seven pieces, which can be combined to create figures and shapes.

Tessellation: An arrangement of shapes that cover an area without gaps or overlaps.

Theory of Everything: A theory that will explain all forces and all matter.

Topology (or rubber-sheet geometry): A branch of mathematics that looks at an object's surfaces, its regions, and connections as the object is bent, squashed, and stretched out of shape without tearing.

Triangle number: (1) A number calculated by totaling positive whole numbers in order; examples include 1, 3, 6, 10, 15, 21. (2) The number of dots needed to make a triangle. The sum of any two consecutive triangle numbers is a square number.

Triangulation: A method to figure out distance using trigonometry, based on the triangle formed by three points.

Trigonometry: A branch of mathematics that explores the relations between sides and angles of triangles, especially right-angled triangles.

Unholey prime: A prime number made up of digits without holes (e.g., 1,117).

Vanishing point: The point at which parallel lines leading off into the distance appear to meet.

Venn diagram: A diagram using circles inside a rectangle to represent sets, or groups of things, and the relationships between these sets.

Volume: The total amount of space inside a 3-D object.

Whole numbers: Natural numbers and zero (e.g., 0, 1, 2, 3).

SELECTED BIBLIOGRAPHY

GENERAL

Chartier, Tim. *Math Bytes: Google Bombs, Chocolate-Covered Pi, and Other Cool Bits in Computing*. Princeton, NJ: Princeton University Press, 2014.

Devlin, Keith. Devlin's Angle, various articles [Internet]. http://www.maa.org/external_archive/devlin/devangle.html.

———. *Life by the Numbers*. New York: John Wiley and Sons, 1998.

Gardner, Martin. *The Colossal Book of Mathematics: Classic Puzzles Paradoxes and Problems*. New York: W.W. Norton, 2007.

Pappas, Theoni. *The Joy of Mathematics*. Rev. ed. San Carlos, CA: Wide World Publishing/Tetra, 1989.

———. *Math Stuff*. San Carlos, CA: Wide World Publishing/Tetra, 2002.

Peterson, Ivars. "MatheMUSEments" articles [Internet] 2007–08. http://musemath.blogspot.ca/.

Stewart, Ian. *Math Hysteria*. New York: Oxford University Press. 2004.

———. "Mathematical Recreations" column, *Scientific American,* 1991–2001.

———. *Professor Stewart's Incredible Numbers*. New York: Basic Books. 2015.

CHAPTER 1

Cintron-Arias, Ariel. *To Go Viral*. arXiv:1402.3499v1 [physics.soc-ph]. [Internet] February 14, 2014. http://arxiv.org/pdf/1402.3499.pdf.

Joyce, Helen. "Natural Born Mathematicians." *Plus Magazine* 19 (March 2002). http://plus.maths.org/issue19/features/butterworth/index.html.

Wynn, Karen (1992). "Addition and Subtraction by Human Infants." *Nature* 358: 749–50.

CHAPTER 2

Gordon, P. "Numerical Cognition without Words: Evidence from Amazonia." *Science* 306 (2004): 496–99.

PBS Mathline. "Activity I: Industrial Design: The Geometry of Bicycle Designs." PBS Learning Media. http://www-tc.pbs.org/teachers/mathline/concepts/designandmath/Act1Solution.pdf

Scientific American. "How Should You Launch a Ball to Achieve the Greatest Distance?" *Scientific American*, November 9, 2010. http://www.scientificamerican.com/article/football-projectile-motion/.

Tran, Chau M. and Larry M. Silverberg. "Optimal Release Conditions for the Free Throw in Men's Basketball." *Journal of Sports Sciences* 26, 11 (2008): 1147–155. doi: 10.1080/02640410802004948.

Wagon, Stan. "The Ultimate Flat Tire." *Math Horizons,* February 1999: 14–17.

CHAPTER 3

Britton, Jill. "Escher in the Classroom" [electronic condensed version]. In *M.C. Escher's Legacy: A Centennial Celebration*, proceedings of the International Escher Congress, Rome, July 1998. Edited by D. Schattschneider and M. Emmer. Berlin: Springer-Verlag, 2003. http://britton.disted.camosun.bc.ca/jbescher.htm.

Criminisi, Antonio, with Rachel Thomas. "Getting into the Picture." *Plus Magazine* 23 (January 2003). https://plus.maths.org/content/issue/23.

Hodgins, Jessica K., and James F O'Brien. "Computer Animation." In *Encyclopedia of Computer Science*. 4th ed. New York: John Wiley and Sons, 2003.

Lang, Robert J. "Origami." [Internet] 2004–16. http://www.langorigami.com.

Linden, Greg, Brent Smith, and Jeremy York. Amazon.com Recommendations: "Item-to-Item Collaborative Filtering, IEEE Internet Computing," v.7 n.1, 76–80. January 2003.

Miyashita, Shuhei, Steven Guitron, Marvin Ludersdorfer, Cynthia R. Sung, and Daniela Rus. "An Untethered Miniature Origami Robot That Self-folds, Walks, Swims, and Degrades." Paper presented at the 2015 International Conference on Robotics and Automation, Seattle, May 2015.

Spring, Tom. "Algorithms That Rule the Web." PC World. [Internet]. http://www.pcworld.com/article/236226/8_Algorithms_That_Rule_Web.html.

Society for Industrial and Applied Mathematics. Google PageRank: "The Mathematics of Google. WhyDoMath." [Internet] http://www.whydomath.org/node/google/math.html.

Thalmann, N. Magnenat and D. Thalmann. "Computer Animation." In Handbook of Computer Science. Edited by Allen B. Tucker. London: Chapman and Hall/CRC Press, 2004.

CHAPTER 4

Benson, Dave. Music: A Mathematical Offering. [Internet] 1995–2006. https://homepages.abdn.ac.uk/mth192/pages/html/music.pdf.

MIDI Manufacturers Association. "Tutorial: The Technology of MIDI." [Internet] http://www.midi.org/aboutmidi/tut_techomidi.php.

NASA. "Black Hole Sound Waves." [Internet], September 9, 2003. http://science.nasa.gov/science-news/science-at-nasa/2003/09sep_blackholesounds/.

Rosenthal, Jeffrey S. "The Mathematics of Music." Plus Magazine 35 (May 2005). http://plus.maths.org/issue35/features/rosenthal/index.html.

Schmidt-Jones, Catherine. "Time Signature." OpenStax CNX. [Internet] February 15, 2013. http://cnx.org/contents/68100121-0efa-4bd8-a0ca-3336e8d01a10@16.

CHAPTER 5

Devlin, Keith. The Math Instinct: Why You're a Mathematical Genius (Along with Lobsters, Birds, Cats and Dogs). New York: Thunder Mouth Press, 2005.

Prabhakar, B., K.N. Dektar, and D.M. Gordon. "The Regulation of Ant Colony Foraging Activity without Spatial Information." PLOS Computational Biology 8, 8 (2012): e1002670. doi:10.1371/journal.pcbi.1002670.

Tarpy, D.R. The Honey Bee Dance Language. Raleigh, NC: North Carolina Cooperative Extension Service, 2004.

Uller, Claudia. "Salamanders (Plethodon cinereus) Go for More: Rudiments of Number in an Amphibian." Animal Cognition 6, 2 (2003): 105–12.

Wehner, R., and M.V. Srinivasan. "Searching Behaviour of Desert Ants Genus Cataglyphis (Formicidae, Hymenoptera)." Journal of Comparative Physiology 142 (1981): 315–38.

CHAPTER 6

Fractal Foundation. Fractal Pack 1 Educator's Guide. (2009). [Internet] http://fractalfoundation.org/fractivities/FractalPacks-EducatorsGuide.pdf.

Stewart, Ian. Nature's Numbers. New York: Basic Books, 1995).

Turner, Martin J. "Modelling Nature with Fractals." Plus Magazine 6 (September 1998). [Internet] http://plus.maths.org/issue6/turner2/index.html.

CHAPTER 7

Levinovitz, Alan. "The Mystery of Go, the Ancient Game That Computers Still Can't Win." [Internet] http://www.wired.com/2014/05/the-world-of-computer-go/.

Olson, R.S. "Here's Waldo: Computing the Optimal Search Strategy for Finding Waldo." [Internet] February 3, 2015. http://www.randalolson.com/2015/02/03/heres-waldo-computing-the-optimal-search-strategy-for-finding-waldo/.

CHAPTER 8

Cesare, C. "Encryption Faces Quantum Foe." *Nature* 525 (September 10, 2015): 167–68.

Devlin, K. "Statisticians Not Wanted." Devlin's Angle. [Internet] September 2006. https://www.maa.org/external_archive/devlin/devlin_09_06.html.

Gardner, Martin. *Penrose Tiles to Trapdoor Ciphers...and the Return of Dr. Matrix*. Rev. ed. Washington, DC: Mathematical Association of America, 1997.

Medeiros, J. "How Geographic Profiling Helps Find Serial Criminals." *Wired*. [Internet] November 10, 2014. http://www.wired.co.uk/magazine/archive/2014/11/features/mapping-murder.

Rivest, R.L., A. Shamir, and L. Adleman. 1978. "A Method for Obtaining Digital Signatures and Public-Key Cryptosystems." *Communications of the ACM* 21, 2 (February 1978): 120–26.

Robinson, Sara. "Still Guarding Secrets after Years of Attacks, RSA Earns Accolades for Its Founders." *SIAM News* 36, 5 (June 2003).

Short, M. "The Math behind the Scene of the Crime." *Physics Today* 67, 1 (2014): 58–59.

CHAPTER 9

Nestler, Andrew, and Sarah J. Greenwald. *Simpsons Math*. [Internet] Retrieved from Appalachian State University Department of Mathematical Sciences website: http://www.mathsci.appstate.edu/~sjg/simpsonsmath/.

Singh, Simon. *The Simpsons and Their Mathematical Secrets*. New York: Bloomsbury, 2013.

BIOGRAPHIES

Deakin, Michael B. "Hypatia and Her Mathematics." *American Mathematical Monthly* 101, 3 (March 1994), 234–43.

Lynch, John (writer and producer), and Simon Singh (director). "The Proof," *NOVA*. Transcript from television program and companion website. BBC/WGBH Boston Co-Production. PBS airdate, October 28, 1997. http://www.pbs.org/wgbh/nova/proof/wiles.html.

Masood, Ehsan. *Science and Islam: A History*. London: Icon Books, 2009.

Singh, Simon. "Math's Hidden Woman." In *Fermat's Enigma: The Epic Quest to Solve the World's Greatest Mathematical Problem*. New York: Walker and Co., 1997. Retrieved from Nova website: http://www.pbs.org/wgbh/nova/proof/germain.html.

Tucker, Liz (director and producer). "Infinite Secrets." *NOVA*. Companion website and transcript. BBC/WGBH Boston Co-Production. PBS airdate September 30, 2003. Retrieved from Nova website: http://www.pbs.org/wgbh/nova/archimedes/about.html and http://www.pbs.org/wgbh/nova/transcripts/3010_archimed.html.

FURTHER READING

NON-FICTION

The Cat in Numberland by Ivar Ekeland, illustrated by John O'Brien (Cricket Books, 2006). Based on mathematician David Hilbert's paradox and featuring an irritated cat, this is a fun exploration of the concept of infinity. Recommended for grades 3 to 5.

G is for Googol: A Math Alphabet Book by David M. Schwartz, illustrated by Marissa Moss (Ten Speed Press, 1998). Covers aspects of mathematics from Abacus to Zillion, stopping in at Googol, Nature and Venn Diagrams along the way. Recommended for grades 3 and up.

Go Figure! A Totally Cool Book About Numbers, by Johnny Ball (DK Children, 2005). A highly visual exploration of a variety of mathematical topics. Recommended for grades 4 and up.

How Much Is a Million? by David M. Schwartz, illustrated by Steven Kellogg (Harper Collins, 2004, first published in 1985). Shows you what huge numbers really look like. Recommended for grades 3 and up.

Mathemagic! by Lynda Colgan, illustrated by Jane Kurisu (Kids Can Press, 2011). Number tricks with step-by-step explanations of the mathematics behind them. Recommended for grades 5 to 9.

Mathematicians Are People Too, Vol. I and *Vol. II* by Luetta and Wilburt Reimer (Dale Seymour Publications, 1990, 1995). Lively stories about famous mathematicians from different times and places and their contributions to the world of mathematics. Recommended for grades 3 to 7.

FICTION

One Grain of Rice: A Mathematical Folktale, by Demi (Scholastic, 1997). A retelling of the classic rice on the chessboard story. Recommended for kindergarten to grade 4.

Alice's Adventures in Wonderland by Lewis Carroll (Macmillan, 1865). More math than you might think in Alice's bizarre journey. Recommended for grades 4 and up.

The Number Devil by Magnus Enzensberger, illustrated by Rotraut Susanne Berner (Henry Holt, 1998). An intriguing story of a young, math-oppressed boy and the irascible Number Devil who appears in his dreams. Recommended for grades 6 and up.

Through the Looking Glass by Lewis Carroll (Macmillan, 1871). Look for more mathematical language in the adventures of Alice, continued. Recommended for grades 4 and up.

INDEX

PHOTO CREDITS

ABOUT THE AUTHORS

CORA LEE is a scientific writer for the biopharmaceutical and medical device industries. She also writes about science for kids and encourages girls to stay in STEM (science, technology, engineering and math). She is the author of *The Great Motion Mission: A Surprising Story of Physics in Everyday Life*. She lives in Vancouver with her family.

GILLIAN O'REILLY is a freelance writer and editor and is the author of *Slangalicious: Where We Got That Crazy Lingo*. She lives in Toronto with her family.

ABOUT THE ILLUSTRATOR

In addition to illustrating more than a dozen children's books, **LIL CRUMP** has created artwork for magazines, T-shirts, greeting cards, posters, and games, as well as paintings for art gallery shows. If there is an empty surface, Lil will draw or paint on it. Lil is the illustrator of *DNA Detective*. Lil lives with her husband, daughter, and yellow dog, creating fun stuff from her studio overlooking St. Margarets Bay in Nova Scotia.

LOOK FOR THESE OTHER GREAT BOOKS FROM ANNICK PRESS

DNA DETECTIVE

By Tanya Lloyd Kyi, illustrated by Lil Crump

PAPERBACK $14.95 / HARDCOVER $24.95

"Highly recommended as an excellent introduction to criminal forensics." —*Resource Links*

"Should be on the shelves of middle school libraries." —*CM Reviews*

FASTER HIGHER SMARTER: BRIGHT IDEAS THAT TRANSFORMED SPORTS

By Simon Shapiro

PAPERBACK $12.95 USD, $14.95 CAD / HARDCOVER $22.95

What do athletes and rocket scientists have in common?

THE GREAT MOTION MISSION: A SURPRISING STORY OF PHYSICS IN EVERYDAY LIFE

By Cora Lee, illustrated by Steve Rolston

PAPERBACK $14.95 / HARDCOVER $24.95

"Introduces a complicated field of study in a lighthearted way." —*Kirkus Reviews*

"The concepts are explained in easy, relatable terms that make the fundamentals of physics clear to any beginner." —*VOYA*